GOD'S RICHES

GOD'S RICHES

A Work-book on the Doctrines of Grace

John Benton and John Peet

THE BANNER OF TRUTH TRUST

THE BANNER OF TRUTH TRUST
3 Murrayfield Road, Edinburgh, EH12 6EL
P.O. Box 621, Carlisle, Pennsylvania 17013, USA

First Banner of Truth Trust edition 1991

Reprinted 1997

ISBN 0 85151 601 7

Printed in Great Britain by
The Bath Press,
Bath.

CONTENTS

INTRODUCTION

It is always very good when people learn the doctrines of God's grace for themselves from the pages of Scripture. Hence the vision for this work-book.

These studies originated as a series of evening sermons at Chertsey Street Baptist Church, Guildford during the Autumn of 1985 and were later turned into work sheets for home Bible studies, which proved very popular. In preparing this material we are both very aware that we are indebted to many people — too numerous to mention — from whom we have learned over the years. However, we do particularly want to acknowledge the great help that the teaching ministries of both Stuart Olyott and Dr Roy Clements have been in clarifying many issues which are touched on in these pages. Most of all we praise our God for such a wonderful gospel of grace in which we can rejoice.

PART ONE

Foundational Principles

STUDY 1
THE BIBLE

We begin by seeing that there are two great partner-principles on which biblical Christianity is founded. In this lesson we look at the first of these.

Principle 1: *All the Bible and only the Bible*

Sometimes you will find this principle, made famous by the Reformers, written in Latin: *Tota Scriptura: Sola Scriptura.*

Why do we need the Bible?

Read Psalm 19:1-4. The universe and the world around us which God has made reveal much about God in a way that is understandable to people of all languages and backgrounds.

What do you think we can learn about God from creation?

____

____

____

Now look up Romans 1:20. What does it say? Write out the verse.

____

____

____

How can we reply to those who say, 'Show me God and then I will believe'? (See Acts 14:17.)

____

____

But even though creation speaks clearly to us about God, leaving us without an excuse for ignoring him, there are two problems.

First, having turned away from God, mankind has now become insensitive to how creation speaks of the Creator God. We should not be surprised if unbelievers hold to a different view of the origin of our world and do not accept what the Bible teaches. In fact we should expect it (Romans 1:21). Read 1 Corinthians 1:21 and 2:14. Many clever people do not believe (though some do!). What do these verses tell us about why they do not believe?

____

____

____

Secondly, although creation speaks about the existence and power of God, it does not speak about that which has become most important to lost and fallen mankind: *salvation* from sin and its effects. It says enough about God to leave people without excuse for not trusting him, but it does not say enough for people to be able to find the Saviour. How does Romans 10:14 make this plain?

____

____

But God, in grace, has revealed himself in his word which has been committed to writing, the Bible, the Holy Scriptures.

Read the following verses: Psalm 19:7, 8; Matthew 4:4; 1 Peter 1:23-25. Write out 2 Timothy 3:15.

____

____

____

What is the Bible?

From Jesus Christ, the Son of God, we learn that we should accept the thirty-nine books of the Old Testament as *the word of God*. If, as Christians, we follow Christ, we must follow him in his assessment of Scripture.

To see how the Lord Jesus Christ referred to and used the Old Testament, look up Matthew 19:4-5; Mark 7:9-13; Luke 24:25-27; John 10:34-36. Which sections of the Old Testament are referred to in these texts?

____

____

The twenty-seven books of the New Testament were written by Christ's apostles and their close associates. Like the Old Testament writers, these men wrote under the special inspiration of God's Spirit, just as Christ had promised. Read, for example, John 14:26 and 16:13. Their writings are placed on the same level as the Old Testament (1 Thessalonians 4:8; 1 Timothy 5:18; 2 Peter 3:16).

Look at 2 Peter 1:21 and 2 Timothy 3:16. What is meant by the inspiration of God's Spirit?

The *whole* Bible is to be received as the Spirit-breathed word of God. According to Jesus the Old Testament is God's infallible revelation to man (Matthew 5:17-18; John 17:17). He further promised that what his apostles would write would be revealed truth (John 14:26; 16:13). This means that we are to accept all the Bible, and not to pick and choose what we like or to disregard bits we may not like or cannot immediately prove!

WHAT OTHER INDICATIONS ARE THERE THAT THE BIBLE IS GOD'S WORD?

There are many 'external' marks of the truthfulness and divine inspiration of the Bible, for example:

— fulfilled prophecies concerning Christ and his church;

— archaeological corroboration of Bible history;

— the powerful transformation of communities and nations in times past through the preaching of the Bible.

But Christians find themselves fully assured that the Bible is the word of God, not primarily through these evidences, but by the witness of the Holy Spirit within them. See 1 John 2:20, 27; 1 Corinthians 14:37.

The external evidences are for all to see, but few people ever come to see their significance. Even before some of the specific evidences came to light Christians believed Scripture to be the word of God. Take God at his word. God is a faithful God who does not lie (Numbers 23:19).

The Puritan Richard Sibbes quotes Salvian concerning the trustworthiness of God: 'Who hath made the earth faithful to bring forth fruit . . . but God? Yet we can trust the ground with sowing our seed. Who makes man faithful, who is by nature the most slippery and unconstant creature of all other, but God only? Yet we can trust a vain man, whose breath is in his nostrils, and look for great matters at his hands, before an all-sufficient God, that changeth not. Who makes the seas and the winds faithful, that they do not hurt us, but God? And yet we are apt to trust the wind and weather sooner than God, as we see many seamen that will thrust forth their goods into the wide ocean in a small bark, to shift any way, rather than trust God with them.' [1]

People naturally, and against all logic, refuse to trust God. But the Holy Spirit convinces the Christian that God is faithful and that his word, the Bible, is trustworthy.

ONLY the Bible

Having received such a book from God:

— we *need* not look anywhere else to find out what to believe, how to behave or how to interpret the experiences of life;

— we *ought* not to look anywhere else, for this is the only infallible source of revelation that God has given us.

1. EVERYTHING WHICH GOD REQUIRES US TO BELIEVE IS FOUND IN THE BIBLE (2 TIMOTHY 3:16-17)

We are not to add to it (that we want to know more does not mean we need to know more), or take away from it (Deuteronomy 4:2; Revelation 22: 18-19).

Anything which goes against the plain teaching of the Bible is false (Galatians 1:8-9).

We must examine everything in the light of the Scriptures (Acts 17:11; 1 John 4:1-2).

These are not popular views. You will always find 'clever men' who 'know' better. How should we react to such people?

2. EVERYTHING WE NEED TO KNOW ABOUT HOW TO BEHAVE IS FOUND IN THE BIBLE

By following its teaching we can become all that God wants us to be. See Psalm 119:9; 2 Timothy 3:15-17; Matthew 7:24-25. The Holy Spirit always guides us in conformity to the Bible (1 Corinthians 14:37-38), and obedience to Scripture brings joy and blessing (Psalm 1:1-3; 19:8; John 14:21, 23).

How should we respond to someone who says, 'But 20th-century culture and conditions are so different from those in Bible times; we can't look to the Bible to tell us how to behave now'?

ALL the Bible

The Bible is God's word. We do not need to look outside it to find out about God or our relationship to him. But we must seek to be well acquainted with *everything* in it.

If we do not know the *whole* of God's word:

1. OUR VIEW OF CHRIST WILL BE DEFECTIVE

Look at Luke 24:25-27, 44. What do your non-Christian friends say about Christ? How do your views differ from theirs?

Compare with Matthew 16:13-17.

2. OUR SPIRITUAL LIVES WILL BE DEFECTIVE

   Read Matthew 4:4; 2 Timothy 3:15-17. What do these verses indicate that we need the Bible for?

   ____

   ____

3. WE BECOME EASY PREY FOR FALSE TEACHERS, ERROR, AND ALL SORTS OF SPECULATION AND MAN-MADE PHILOSOPHIES

   Read Mark 12:24; Colossians 2:8.

   Note: The false sects and religions all depend on some so-called revelation other than the Bible. So, beware!

We should give our closest attention to *all* the Bible (2 Timothy 3:16; *cf.* Psalm 119:9; Romans 15:4). We must give the Bible a central position in the church and in the Christian life. Beware of any church that neglects the Bible.

We seek to give the Bible a central place:

1. By giving priority to the public reading of Scripture in the church as we meet (1 Timothy 4:13).

2. By giving priority to expository preaching and teaching. Expository preaching and teaching is that which seeks to proclaim the content of the Bible by carefully considering its meaning both in the immediate context of the passage and in the context of the Bible as a whole, and applying its truth to our lives. In this way every member of the congregation becomes acquainted with the whole word and will of God (Acts 20:27). What are the advantages of expository preaching over the preaching of isolated texts of Scripture?

   ____

   ____

3. By giving priority to the reading of Scripture and meditating upon it in our personal daily devotions (Psalm 1:2).

   What would be your response to those who say that the Bible is too difficult for you to study by yourself?

   ____

   ____

   ____

Conclusion

In a sentence or two, state what you have learned from this study.

____

____

____

____

Is there any resolution or prayer that, God helping you, this study has challenged you to make?

____

____

____

STUDY 2
GLORY TO GOD ALONE

The Bible is a book primarily concerned with revealing the true and living God. This study deals with the second of the two great partner-principles on which biblical Christianity is founded.

Principle 2: *Glory to God alone*

The message of the Bible is very different from that of modern, atheistic philosophy. Holding that there is no God and that our world and all that is in it, including ourselves, are merely the products of blind chance, leads people to the rather depressing view that our lives are ultimately pointless and meaningless.

The message of the Bible is diametrically opposed to this view of life. It tells us that God is there, that he is the centre of all things, and that he has created the world and is unfolding history with the purpose that glory should be brought to his great name through Jesus Christ our Lord (Ephesians 1:6, 14; 3:20-21; Philippians 2:10-11; Jude 25).

Without God, self becomes our god.

The book of Revelation shows us that the consummation of history will be the praise and worship of God in the new heavens and earth. Write out the song of worship found in Revelation 5:13.

____

____

____

The message of the Bible for us *now* is that our lives are to be lived for the glory of God (Mark 12:28-30).

On first sight this might appear selfish of God. But it is not. First of all, the glory rightfully belongs to God. In particular, history is moving to its climax in the second coming of Christ. Then it will be clearly seen and acknowledged by all that it is right and as it should be that Jesus Christ is Lord. '*Worthy* is the Lamb that was slain' is the song of heaven. Secondly, as his creatures glorify God, they themselves are blessed. It is to God's glory that we find joy and peace in *his* service. It is through glorifying God that his creation finds fulfilment. Look, for example, at Psalm 96:11-13. Notice how the coming of the Lord brings well-being to the world. His presence brings light and joy. He is the Lord who makes everything sing with delight.

Biblical Christianity is all about God and his glory. Many perversions of Christianity start with man, thereby, in fact, exalting man above God. Inevitably they lead to a truncated and distorted faith at best, and at worst they end up in chaos, reducing God to man's lackey.

This principle of glory to God alone was expressed at the Reformation by the Latin phrase *soli Deo gloria*.

It is essential that you look up the references given below to make sure that this *is* what the Bible teaches about God. We will consider who God is, and then what God has done. This will lead us on to see why glory must be his alone.

Who God IS

1. THE BEING OF GOD

   Consider each of these aspects of the nature of God and reflect on how different we are from him. God is:

Spirit	John 4:24
invisible	John 1:18; 1 Timothy 6:16
personal	Malachi 2:10; John 14:9, 23
infinite — everywhere present	Psalm 139:7-10; Jeremiah 23:23-24
eternal	Psalm 90:2; 102:27
all-knowing	Psalm 139:2-5; Hebrews 4:13
incomprehensible	Job 11:7; Isaiah 40:18
unsearchable	Isaiah 40:13-14; Romans 11:33-34
all-sufficient	Exodus 3:14; John 5:26
sovereign	Daniel 4:34-35; Ephesians 1:11

   Many people, faced with such an awe-inspiring list of the attributes of God, would think that God is 'way out there' and so distant from us as to be irrelevant to us or unconcerned about us. Look again at the list. Why can Christians take delight in each of these attributes of God?

2. THE CHARACTER OF GOD

God is:

holy	Exodus 15:11; Isaiah 6:3
righteous	Psalm 97:2; 145:17
loving	1 John 4:8, 10, 16
good	Psalm 86:5; 107:1
wise	Psalm 104:24; Daniel 2:20
unchanging	Malachi 3:6; James 1:17

A common statement made by non-Christians is, 'God is love and so he should not do such and such a thing or allow it to happen.' What is wrong with that kind of statement?

____

____

____

How, then, does God's whole character work for the good of his people?

____

____

3. GOD IS TRINITY

The Bible teaches that there are three Persons in the Godhead: the Father, the Son (Jesus Christ) and the Holy Spirit. These three are the one true eternal God, the same in substance, equal in power and glory, although distinguished by their personal properties.

Read carefully Matthew 3:16-17; 28:19; John 10:30; 2 Corinthians 13:14. How do these texts justify the statements made in the last paragraph?

____

____

____

____

Note: Before you try to explain this to anyone, remember (from what we have already seen) that God is ultimately incomprehensible to us. Do not try to reduce him to human logic. He is above that. He is unique. He is God.

Why not pause (if you have not already done so) and revel in the things you have just learned or been reminded of about God and worship him? We are to glorify God for what he is (Psalm 48:1).

What God has DONE

God is the God who has acted and who acts. He is the God of:

1. CREATION

   Read carefully Genesis 1:1-31; Hebrews 11:3.

   We were created by him, so let us give him the glory due to him (Psalm 95:6). Our very existence is dependent on him (Acts 17:28) — so how foolish to try to live without him!

   There are many people who try to explain the existence of the world without reference to God. Why do you believe differently from them?

   ____

   ____

   ____

   See what the Bible says about such people (Psalm 53:1).

2. PROVIDENCE

   Look at Psalm 103:19; 145:16; Romans 11:36. God is in control of all that goes on in the world. We are provided for by God. So let us give glory to him. We will look a little more carefully at this in the next lesson. Meanwhile just think through some of his provisions for us. The list is long — just note a sample.

   ____

   ____

   ____

   ____

3. JUDGMENT

   Read the following: Ecclesiastes 12:14; Hebrews 9:27; Revelation 20:11-15. God will see that justice is done for all the wrongs in the world. He will judge us righteously. So let us give him glory that he is a just Judge (Psalm 98:9). How would you answer the person who says that God does nothing about the evil in the world?

   ____

   ____

   ____

4. REDEMPTION

Carefully read these passages of Scripture: John 3:16; Romans 3:24-25; 8:3-4; 2 Corinthians 4:6. If you are a Christian it is because God has redeemed you. So let us give glory to him (Ephesians 1:3). The word 'redemption' implies a price that has been paid. What price was paid for our redemption? See 1 Peter 1:18-19.

____

____

Glory to God ALONE

We are to thank people who are kind to us in our daily lives, but we must realize that behind their kindness is the kindness of God. Without God that person would not have been there to show us kindness, or have had a kind inclination towards us. We are to thank the people who led us to Christ. But we are to realize that behind what they did, ultimately, was the activity of God.

So, while it is absolutely right to thank others, the true glory is for God *alone*. He is the only object of our worship.

If God is responsible for the kindness we meet in other people, what would the world be like if God withdrew his Spirit and his common grace?

____

____

There is *no other* God. Look up Deuteronomy 6:4; Psalm 18:31; Isaiah 45:21; 1 Corinthians 8:4. So we should give worship to him alone.

Is it possible for civilized, sophisticated 20th-century people to worship other 'gods'? If so, what are these gods?

____

____

1. *Creation* is entirely God's work (Job 38:4-11; Isaiah 44:24; Revelation 4:11). He did it alone. Therefore we should give the glory to him alone for creation.

   How do some people try to minimize, or eliminate, God's activity in creation?

   ____

   ____

   ____

2. *Providence* is, ultimately, entirely God's work. Read Romans 11:36; Psalm 135:6; Matthew 10:29. We are to give him alone the glory. Beware the modern tendency to give credit to 'coincidence', 'good luck' and 'Nature', as, for example, when people say, 'I had a lucky escape' or 'Hasn't Nature arranged things marvellously?' What does this tell you about the spiritual sensitivity of unredeemed people?

   ____

   ____

3. *Judgment* is entirely in the hands of God (Acts 17:31; Romans 2:5-11, 16; Revelation 20:11-13). We are to give him alone the glory.

   Look at Romans 12:17-20. How should the fact that it is for God to judge affect our everyday lives?

   ____

   ____

   ____

   We should thank God that he, rather than anyone else, is our Judge.

4. *Redemption* is entirely the work of God. We take no credit whatsoever for our salvation. All boasting or self-congratulation is excluded (Romans 3:27; 1 Corinthians 4:7). We are his workmanship (Ephesians 2:8-10). In heaven people give the glory to God alone for their salvation. Write out Revelation 7:10.

   ____

   ____

Conclusion

Why can we say that the descriptions of God given in this study are all true of Jesus Christ and of the Holy Spirit as well as of the Father?

____

____

____

What have you learned about God from this lesson which will help you in your daily life?

____

____

____

Thomas Watson reminds us: 'We glorify God by walking cheerfully. It brings glory to God, when the world sees a Christian has that within him that can make him cheerful in the worst times; that can enable him, with the nightingale, to sing with a thorn at his breast. The people of God have ground for cheerfulness. They are justified and adopted, and this creates inward peace; it makes music within, whatever storms are without. 2 Corinthians 1:4. 1 Thessalonians 1:6. If we consider what Christ has wrought for us by his blood, and wrought in us by his Spirit, it is a ground of great cheerfulness, and this cheerfulness glorifies God. It reflects upon a master when the servant is always drooping and sad ... A Christian's cheerful looks glorify God; religion does not take away our joy, but refines it; it does not break our viol, but tunes it, and makes the music sweeter.' [2]

STUDY 3
GOD'S SOVEREIGNTY AND MAN'S RESPONSIBILITY

In the last study, where we considered the truth that glory is for God alone, we said in discussing his work of providence that ultimately God is in control of all that goes on in the world. We also spoke of God judging the world. When these truths are taken together, a question arises in our minds: 'If God is in control of everything, how can people be held responsible for the things they do?' It would seem that either God is not in control of absolutely everything, or he is unfair to judge us. In this study we investigate what the Bible has to say about God's sovereignty and human responsibility.

GOD'S SOVEREIGNTY

By this we mean God's supreme and detailed control over all that comes to pass in heaven and on earth.

Read Daniel 4:35. The circumstances are significant. Who was the king who spoke these words?

Do you remember the story of how he became very proud, believing that his great achievements were all his own doing? God humbled him (Daniel 4:24-25), and took away his sovereignty until he acknowledged that God was the King (Daniel 4:31-32).

Read Romans 11:36. Of what does the apostle Paul say that God is the beginning, the sustainer and the end?

The Bible speaks specifically of God foreordaining everything that comes to pass.

Look at Ephesians 1:11. What does God work out according to the purpose of his will?

Look at Ephesians 1:6, 12. What is the purpose of his planning?

HUMAN RESPONSIBILITY

By this we mean that our actions and our choices are our own and we are morally accountable to God. People are not mere puppets or robots.

Read Ezekiel 33:1-9. In these verses we read of God holding two groups of people responsible before him. Sinners are responsible for their sins and the prophet/watchman is responsible to warn the people of the coming judgment of God. How does verse 6 speak of the prophet's accountability?

Read Acts 10:1-4. Not only does God hold us responsible for our sins but he also recognizes our responsibility for acts of generosity and kindness.

Read 2 Corinthians 5:10 and Revelation 20:11-13. Who are to stand before God to be judged, according to these verses?

Because of fallen man's spiritual blindness he does not like talk of God's sovereignty and man's responsibility (he prefers to think of man's sovereignty and God's responsibility). But, as we have seen, the Bible teaches these truths.

Let us next try to see how these two truths are related.

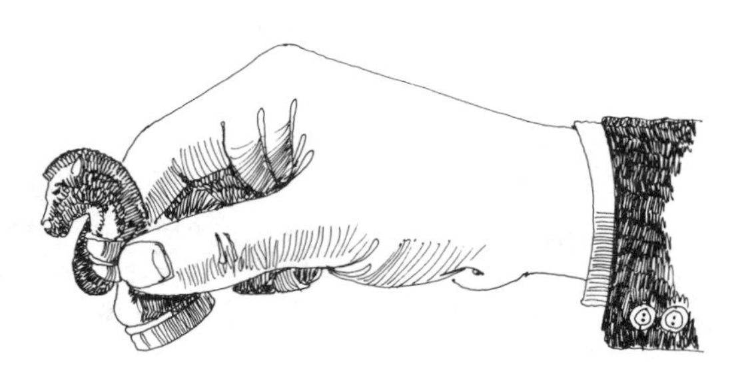

God is in control of all that goes on in our world.

A survey of some Bible texts

1. SOME EXAMPLES OF GOD'S SOVEREIGNTY AND *SINFUL* HUMAN ACTIONS

   Joseph. Read Genesis 37:26-28 and 50:20. What Joseph's brothers did to him was wicked, yet it furthered God's plan. Consider Genesis 50:21. What was Joseph's attitude?

   David. Look up 2 Samuel 24:1, 10 and 1 Chronicles 21:1. Here is a remarkable synthesis of God's sovereignty, Satanic activity and human responsibility. Write down the statements which draw attention to the activity of God, Satan and David.

Christ's death. At the cross, God's plan was precisely fulfilled, yet Judas and those who crucified the Lord Jesus are held responsible for this wicked act. Read Luke 22:22 and write down the phrase describing God's action and the phrase describing man's responsibility.

Now read Acts 2:23, where Peter speaks about the events of the cross. Write down the phrase for God's action and the phrase which describes man's responsibility.

2. SOME EXAMPLES OF GOD'S SOVEREIGNTY AND *GOOD* HUMAN ACTIONS

Coming to Christ. We are responsible to repent and believe the gospel (Matthew 11:20-24; Acts 2:37-38). Look up Matthew 11:28; John 7:37; Revelation 22:17. To whom are the invitations to salvation made?

Yet we are also told by Jesus that it is only God who enables people to come to Christ. Read John 6:37, 44. What is the promise in verse 37?

How can the person who feels drawn to Christ be encouraged by what the Lord says in verse 44?

Living as Christians. We are responsible to make the effort to live as Christians should, hence we find many commands to Christians in the New

Testament (1 Peter 1:13-15). Yet as we respond positively and obey, it is God working within us, says the Bible. Look up Philippians 2:12-13. Note that the verses say that God accomplishes everything he wants to do.

Persevering in the Christian life. Read Jude verses 1, 21 and 24. What verb concerning perseverance and preservation in the Christian life is used both of ourselves and of God in these verses?

We must keep ourselves, yet all the time we are kept by God.

From this short survey, it begins to emerge that the Bible teaches both God's sovereignty and man's responsibility. They are separate things and yet they are coincident realities.

This may appear illogical to us, with our finite understanding. If God is totally in control, we tend to think that would lead to a determinism which leaves man as a non-responsible puppet. On the other hand, if we start with man's responsibility before God, we tend to think that he must have free will in such a way that God can only do so much and no more.

But the Bible does not teach either of these things. It teaches man's total responsibility and God's complete sovereignty at the same time, without compromising either.

The logical necessity for both

God's sovereignty is necessary to his being and holiness. If there is something over which God cannot rule, then he is not truly God. Further, it would be immoral of God either to choose not to control or to have made a universe which he could not control.

> *B. B Warfield writes: 'A God who could or would make a creature whom he could not or would not control, is no God . . . He would have ceased to be a moral being. It is an immoral act to make a thing that we cannot or will not control. The only justification for making anything is that we both can and will control it. If a man should manufacture a quantity of an unstable high-explosive in the corridors of an orphanage and when the stuff went off should seek to excuse himself by saying that he could not control it, no one would count his excuse as valid. What right had he to manufacture it, we would say, unless he could control it? He relieves himself of none of the responsibility for the havoc wrought by pleading inability to control his creation. To suppose that God has made a universe — or even a single being — the control of which he renounces, is to accuse him of similar immorality.'* [3]

There is a similar logical necessity of real human responsibility and freedom. The whole of Christianity presupposes human responsibility. Unless there is a voluntary element in love, for example, love is not love and God is not truly loved by his people. Read Matthew 22:37 and note that our love is active and is the response of our whole being. For a human being to say sincerely, 'I love you' is one thing, but the same words coming from the mouth of a robot which has been programmed to repeat the phrase are completely different.

Thus we see that both God's total sovereignty and man's real responsibility are logically necessary and taught by the Scriptures, although we cannot fathom how they ultimately fit together. We have to be content to realize that God, and the relationship which he bears to the world, are greater than we can understand.

The great theologian Augustine of Hippo (354-430), put it succinctly. He said, 'Dogma is but the fence around the mystery.' In other words, the Scriptures keep us from wandering into error, but although they give us the truth, they cannot give us the full truth, for God is greater than our limited understanding can comprehend. There are certain things which we believe although we cannot fully understand or explain them. The relationship between God's sovereignty and human responsibility is one of these things.

Scripture truth is the fence that protects us.

Keeping the balance

1. GOD AND THE PROBLEM OF EVIL

   We have seen from the examples of Joseph, David, and the cross of Christ, that evil cannot break out of the sphere of divine sovereignty. Evil never dethrones God. In some sense, God stands behind both good and evil (Isaiah 54:16). But, we must insist, he does not stand behind them both in the same way. Although it is not outside his control, God is not the author of evil, nor can we shift the blame for evil on to him. Look at Job 1:10-12. According to this passage who incited Job to sin?

____

Now look at James 1:17. Who is the author of all good gifts?

____

2. GOD AND PRAYER

The Bible stresses God's predestination and sovereignty, but it has a high view also of the effectiveness of the Christian's prayers. Prayer is so effective that some Christians have spoken of it as God's trumpet heralding the fact that he is about to do something. God does nothing without setting his people praying for it first. That is one way to view the effectiveness of prayer.

Secondly, prayer is so effective that it is not wrong for us, from our finite perspective, to picture prayer as capable of affecting God's will. Read Genesis 18:22-33. What was Abraham's prayer?

____

____

What was God's response?

____

____

Read Isaiah 38:1-6. Through Christ, God actually takes notice of us. We must not lose hold of that. At the same time, the very reason we pray is because we believe God is sovereign and therefore is able to answer us.

Look up Jeremiah 32:17, 26-27. Why can we bring anything to God in prayer?

____

____

3. GOD AND EVANGELISM

God's sovereignty in saving people (Acts 16:14) is not an excuse for us to sit back and do nothing in the belief that 'If God is going to save people he does not need me to help him.' God's sovereignty and our responsibility to preach the gospel go hand in hand. God's sovereignty should be an encouragement to us to get on with the hard work of evangelism. This is how it worked both for the Lord Jesus (Matthew 11:25-30) and for Paul (Acts 18:9-11). Keep the balance. God's sovereignty means that we can trust him to bring about results. Our responsibility is to do all that we can.

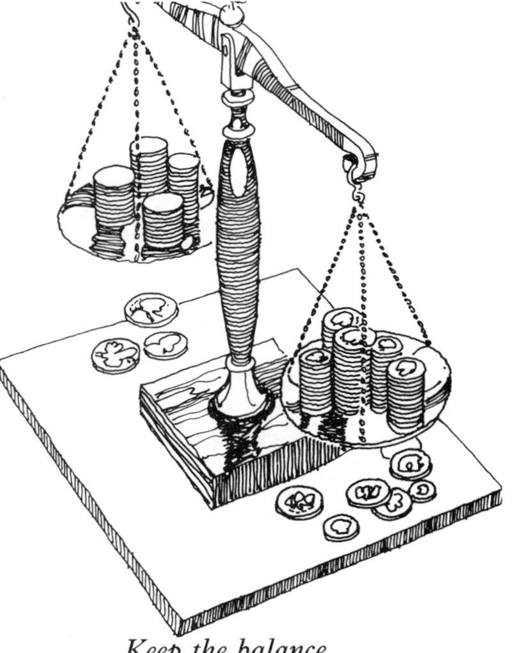
Keep the balance.

4. GOD AND YOUR SALVATION

Together the doctrines of human responsibility and God's sovereignty are a tremendous encouragement to anyone seeking Christ. You have heard the gospel. Now it is your responsibility to repent and believe. You must come to that decision. But as you turn from your old life and follow Christ, it is encouraging to know that it is God working in you to do that, and that the work that God has started he will finish (Philippians 1:6).

What did the Lord say is your responsibility, in Mark 1:15?

But, you may say, you feel too weak to break with your sins and you do not have the power to keep believing. If that is the case, realize that God is sovereign and gracious and that he can supply you with power. He can give you real repentance and faith and keep you on the Christian path. Read Ephesians 2:8 and 1 Peter 1:3.

Believe him. Trust him.

Commenting on the soldiers fulfilling the Old Testament prophecies on the death of Christ (see John 19:31-37), the great 19th-century Baptist preacher, C. H. Spurgeon, comments: 'Shall we never be able to drive into men's minds the truth that predestination and free agency are both facts? Men sin as freely as birds fly in the air, and they are altogether responsible for their sin; and yet everything is ordained and foreseen of God. The fore-ordination of God in no degree interferes with the responsibility of man. I have often been asked by persons to reconcile the two truths. My only reply is — They need no reconciliation, for they never fell out. Why should I try to reconcile two friends? Prove to me that the two truths do not agree. In that request I have set you a task as difficult as that which you propose to me. These two facts are parallel lines; I cannot make them unite, but you cannot make them cross each other. Permit me also to add that I have long ago given up the idea of making all my beliefs into a system. I believe, but I cannot explain. I fall before the majesty of revelation and adore the infinite Lord.' [4]

PART TWO

The Doctrines of God's Grace

STUDY 4
WHAT IS MAN?

David, the psalmist, asked the question which we have chosen as the title of this study. He said, 'When I consider your heavens, the work of your fingers, the moon and the stars, which you have set in place, what is man that you are mindful of him, the son of man that you care for him?' (Psalm 8:3-4). It was a cause of great amazement to David that the God of all majesty should be interested in the human race.

In the first three studies we saw that the Bible is God's book and that it primarily reveals to us the sovereign God and his glory. But it is also the book which tells us the answer to the psalmist's question, 'What is man?' We must understand man and his needs in order to understand what God had graciously to do in order to achieve man's salvation.

GOD CREATED ADAM IN HIS OWN IMAGE AND LIKENESS

Genesis chapter 1 is the divinely inspired account of the creation of the world. We read of the creation of night and day, the oceans and the land, the vegetation, the fish, the birds and the animals. We repeatedly read the formula, 'And God said, Let there be .... And it was so.' However, when Genesis 1 records the creation of man, that formula is strikingly broken. It is no longer just 'Let there be man ...', but rather, as it were, God first pauses and takes counsel within himself, 'Let us make man ...'. Similarly, as Genesis 1 records the creation of the different species, there is the repeated formula that they were made 'according to their kinds', in other words according to the pattern which God had determined. But when it comes to the creation of man the formula is again broken. It is not 'Let us make man ... and God made man according to his kind'. Rather we read, 'God said, Let us make man in our image.' God himself was the blueprint on which the man and the woman were patterned! Read Genesis 1:26-27 carefully. This passage is fundamental to our study. The creation of humanity was the climax of creation.

Take note of the following points and check them by looking up the Bible references. When Adam was created:

— he was a body and spirit from the very beginning (Genesis 2:7);
— he was placed at once in an exalted position (Genesis 1:28);
— he was a righteous, moral creature (Genesis 1:31; Ecclesiastes 7:29);
— he was a spiritual creature who could experience fellowship with God (Genesis 2:7, 15-18);
— he was a personal creature, made for relationships with others (Genesis 2:18, 22-24);
— he was a creature who need never die (Genesis 2:17).

Modern science classifies man simply as 'an animal' who is part of an evolutionary chain. Does the Bible support this classification of man?

____

See 1 Corinthians 15:39 for an interesting commentary on this point.

Man is fundamentally spiritual. He is made in the image of God. He has needs and aspirations different from all other creatures. How do man's unique needs and spiritual aspirations show themselves in the modern world?

____

____

____

Look at Acts 17:16 to see how some of those aspirations were manifested in Athens in Paul's day.

GOD ENTERED INTO A COVENANT WITH ADAM

Covenant is a word used regularly in the Scriptures. It basically means a binding commitment.

Genesis chapter 2 is striking for its introduction of the covenant name of God: the LORD. (It is the personal name of God, not just his title but his name. God used that name in particular when he entered into a covenant with his people. See Exodus 20:2.) Even if the word 'covenant' is not used in this chapter, the first covenant between God and man nevertheless appears here in outline.

Within the covenant of Eden, God gave Adam and Eve many privileges. Check them through for yourself.

— He put them in paradise ('Eden' comes from the Hebrew for 'delight'; Genesis 2:8).
— He gave them fulfilling work to do and the fruits of Eden to eat (Genesis 2:15-16).

— No riches of any sort were lacking for Adam and Eve (Genesis 2:9-14).

— The creatures were placed under man's dominion and care (Genesis 2:19-20).

— The blessing of marriage was given for companionship and comfort (Genesis 2:18, 22-24).

— The day of rest was given in Eden (Genesis 2:2-3).

— Man and woman enjoyed life and fellowship with God. There was no guilt or shame in Eden (Genesis 2:25).

The Bible sees Eden as a foretaste of heaven (compare Genesis 2:9 with Revelation 22:2). How, then, do these points tell us that heaven will be a fulfilling and exciting experience?

____

____

____

____

These were all gifts of God's covenant kindness to Adam. But there was also man's side of the covenant.

God gave man immense freedom (see Genesis 2:16), but he also required certain things of Adam and Eve, and especially of Adam as the head of humanity and of creation. God required personal, perfect and perpetual obedience to himself. That obedience was particularly tested by God's forbidding the man and the woman to eat fruit from the tree of the knowledge of good and evil on pain of death (Genesis 2:16-17).

Why would Adam and Eve initially have found it no burden and much easier to obey God than we do?

____

____

____

The tempter, who is Satan (Revelation 12:9; 20:2), sowed seeds of doubt, unbelief and pride in Eve's mind (Genesis 3:1, 4-5).

Eve was deceived. Adam, standing beside her, chose to break God's clear commandment (Genesis 3:6). He fell into sin.

Do you find any similarity in Satan's approach with Eve and that which he has used ever since? Compare Luke 4:1-13; 1 John 2:16. What are the similarities?

Adam and Eve were persuaded by Satan that God would not actually keep his word. Richard Baxter in his Call to the Unconverted *warns us of the devil preaching the 'mercy' of God: 'The devil's word is, "You may be saved without being born again and converted; you may do well enough without being holy, God doth but frighten you; he is more merciful than to do as he saith, he will be better to you than his word." And, alas, the greatest part of the world believe this word of the devil before the word of God; just as our sin and misery came into the world. God said to our first parents, "If ye eat ye shall die"; and the devil contradicted him, and said, "Ye shall not die": and the woman believed the devil before God. So now the Lord saith, Turn or die: and the devil saith, You shall not die, if you do but cry for God's mercy at last, and give over the acts of sin when you can practise it no longer. And this is the word that the world believes.'* [5]

So sin entered the world. Mankind became guilty and ashamed (Genesis 3:10). They came under the power of death (Romans 5:12), and were afflicted and exposed to many troubles (Genesis 3:14-24). They were expelled from paradise and lost the fellowship with God which they had known before (Genesis 3:23-24).

Give a brief summary of the changes brought about in the world at God's command and as a punishment for sin.

ADAM'S SIN HAS HAD PERMANENT CONSEQUENCES FOR THE WHOLE HUMAN RACE

The covenant was made with Adam as the representative head of the whole human race. As the father of mankind he stood as a representative not only of himself, but of all his descendants. *All* of us sinned in him and fell with him (Acts 17:26; Romans 5:12-19; 1 Corinthians 15:22).

People today like to think of mankind as made up of separate individuals, rather like separate stalks in a field of corn. If one stalk is broken and falls it has little or no effect on any of the others. But that is not the way the Bible pictures mankind. Since Adam was the representative of the whole race, his actions affect us too. His fall is our fall. Furthermore, since we are all descended from Adam the Scriptures picture mankind more as a tree (we speak of family trees, for example): Adam is the trunk of the tree and the rest of mankind are the branches and twigs which grow out of the trunk. But unlike the field of grain, when the trunk of a tree is broken and falls, all the rest — the branches, the twigs and everything — falls with it. This is what has happened to mankind in Adam.

How is the Bible's teaching that all mankind fell in Adam borne out by our observations of everyday life?

___

___

___

All people are now sinners, not simply by imitation but *by nature*. We do not commit sins by accident, or even by some unbiased choice. We commit sins because our very nature has been corrupted by sin (Psalm 51:5; Jeremiah 17:9; Mark 7:20-23; Romans 7:18; Ephesians 2:3).

What is the implication of this for our being made right with God? For example, is forgiveness all we need?

___

___

See John 3:3, 5-6.

That we are all sinners does not mean that we are all as wicked as we could possibly be. Nor does it mean that we cannot be kind, merciful or neighbourly. Something of the image of God remains in us. But because man's whole nature is now tainted with sin, he is altogether unacceptable to a holy God and unable to do anything which pleases him (Romans 8:8).

How does this contrast with the popular view of man?

____

____

____

We are out of touch with God (Genesis 3:24; Ephesians 2:12).

We are under God's anger (Romans 1:18; Ephesians 2:3).

We are in slavery to sin and to Satan (John 8:34; Ephesians 2:2; Romans 6:16-20).

We have a heart which naturally rejects God (Romans 8:7; James 4:4).

All that people have to do to end up in hell is to remain as they are (Luke 16:22-26; 2 Thessalonians 1:9; Revelation 20:12-15; 21:8).

In short, we are hopelessly lost and can do nothing about it (Job 14:14; Jeremiah 13:23; John 3:6a).

We have to face these distressing truths because a wrong diagnosis will lead to a wrong prescription for the cure. The conclusion is that *only* God can save us. There is absolutely no possibility of our saving ourselves. We will consider this in more detail in the next study.

Are you right with God?

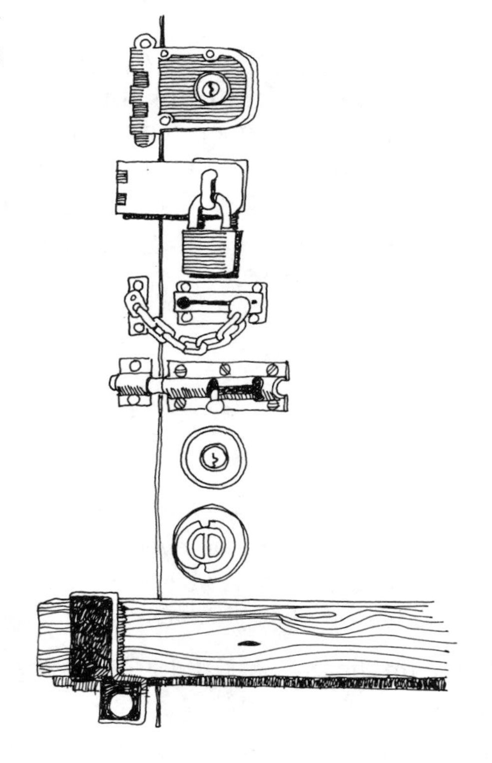

Imprisoned by sin.

Conclusion

How does man today differ from man as God created him?

____

____

____

____

When we consider the terrible matter of sin and its consequences we are caused to wonder afresh with David at our opening question, 'What is man that [God is] mindful of him?' More, perhaps, we should ask, 'Who is this wonderful God that he should still care for us and love us?'

STUDY 5
WHAT HAS HAPPENED TO MAN?

Adam's expulsion from the garden of Eden gave geographical expression to our spiritual separation from God as a consequence of Adam's fall into sin. Sin, as we explained in the last study, has affected all people.

Write out Romans 3:23.

In this study we look more carefully into what the Bible teaches about the results of the Fall of Adam in the life of an individual person. Sin has not left man as it found him. It has changed him profoundly.

What has happened to man himself?

The arrival of sin has damaged and spoiled every area of the individual's life and personality. Through sin our bodies are now exposed to pain and ageing, and death reigns over us. But this is not all. The inner man has also been affected and corrupted.

Inwardly a man has his mind, his will and his affections. Sometimes we speak of the 'heart' of man when we think of the inner man. According to Scripture the whole of the inward man has been tainted by sin.

1. MAN'S MIND AND THINKING HAVE BECOME DARKENED

   This is spelled out for us in verses like Genesis 6:5; Romans 1:28; Ephesians 4:18.

   So, do not be surprised or exasperated when a non-Christian says to you,

'I don't understand', when you speak about Christ to him or her. What should you do?

See Ephesians 1:18.

2. MAN'S WILL AND CHOOSING HAVE BECOME ENSLAVED

   Read the following verses of Scripture: Romans 6:16, 20; Galatians 3:22; Jeremiah 13:23.

   What is the implication of this for the person who says, 'I'll become a Christian when I want to, at some other time'?

---

3. MAN'S EMOTIONS AND DESIRES HAVE BECOME CORRUPTED (Romans 1:24-27; 2 Timothy 3:4, 6).

   What would you say to someone who was going against the laws of God and justifying what they were doing by saying, 'How can something that feels so good be wrong?'?

---

4. THUS MAN'S OUTWARD BEHAVIOUR, WHICH FLOWS FROM HIS THINKING, CHOOSING AND DESIRING, IS NATURALLY POLLUTED IN THE SIGHT OF GOD

   See Mark 7:20-23; Galatians 5:19-21.

The effect of sin on man's nature is often called 'total depravity'. We have seen that this does not mean that man is as wicked as he could possibly be; but it does mean that there is no aspect or area of our nature that is not tainted and defiled by sin.

What has happened to man's relationship to God?

The fellowship and friendship which man knew with God before the Fall in Eden has been completely destroyed.

1. MAN IS HOSTILE TOWARDS GOD (Romans 1:30; 8:7; James 4:4).

   With all the religion there is in the world one might think this could not be true. But the real attitude of the unconverted heart was exposed at Calvary where worldly men crucified the Son of God.

   Before you became a Christian, how did you display this hostility?

   ____

   ____

   ____

2. MAN IS GUILTY BEFORE GOD'S HOLY LAW (Romans 2:12; 3:19-20; Galatians 3:10).
3. MAN IS UNDER GOD'S WRATH (John 3:36; Romans 1:18).
4. MAN IS 'DEAD' IN SINS (Ephesians 2:1-5; Colossians 2:13).

   What are the characteristics of a dead person? How do those characteristics help us to understand what it is to be spiritually dead?

   ____

   ____

   ____

   Look up Genesis 2:17; Ezekiel 37:1-3, 11.

5. MAN'S 'GOOD' WORKS ARE TOTALLY UNAVAILING BECAUSE OF SIN (Isaiah 64:6; Philippians 3:4-9).

   Man likes to think he can earn his salvation. How does this view compare with the biblical diagnosis of man's spiritual condition before God?

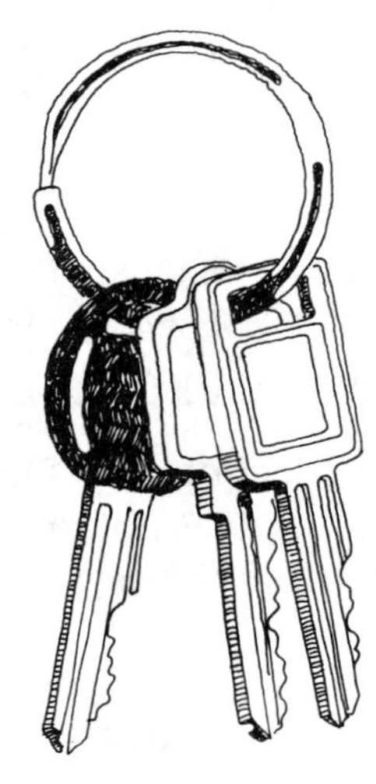

   ____

   ____

   ____

   ____

   ____

Only God holds the keys to our salvation.

While preaching on John 6:32 and commenting on the fact that we are saved by grace not by works, the great reformer Martin Luther said: 'Thus the sum and substance of all doctrine is this, that we are not justified by any works, but that faith in Christ saves. This text is a veritable thunderclap that impels you to exclaim: What can my life and my good works help me? Moses does not aid me. Moses is only a schoolmaster in this field; he instructs me about an external mode of divine service and the strictest outward decency. The works of Moses do not give life and salvation. Here we are informed of another and better bread, called God's bread, which comes from heaven and is not baked on earth. It is granted by the Holy Spirit. It confers everlasting life, a life not merited and earned, a gift from heaven.

Thus you see two kinds of bread here. The one is not earned, not acquired through a self-chosen, self-devised mode of life, but is an outright gift of bread, food, and life. The other is the bread that man wants to merit through good works and the observance of Moses' Law. But whoever refuses to accept life by grace and without merit will never obtain it. The Father gives it; therefore it is not merited. It is mine by sheer mercy and grace. Thus my merit is toppled over and knocked to the ground.' [6]

What happens when man hears the gospel?

The gospel of the Lord Jesus Christ is good news for us sinners. But without the work of the Holy Spirit in our hearts that is not how man responds to it! When he hears it:

1. MAN CONTINUES TO SUPPRESS THE TRUTH (John 9:24-34; Acts 18:5-6; Romans 1:18, 21).

   Why does man do this?

   ____

   ____

   ____

2. MAN DOES NOT UNDERSTAND IT (Matthew 13:19; John 3:5-10; 1 Corinthians 2:14).

   Man misunderstands it, reinterpreting it in terms of his own preconceived ideas. For an example of this look at what happened to Paul and Barnabas when they preached the gospel in Lystra (Acts 14:8-18).

   How does popular modern psychology interpret the gospel and its effects?

   ____

   ____

   ____

3. MAN DISCOUNTS THE PROVISIONS OF THE GOSPEL AS FOOLISH AND WORTHLESS (1 Corinthians 1:18-25; John 18:37-38).

All this helps us to understand why evangelism is hard work! Look at 2 Corinthians 4:1-6 and find some of the truths which encouraged Paul to continue in his evangelistic efforts.

____

____

____

____

What needs to happen to man for him to receive the gospel?

In order to be saved, in order to receive Christ, a person must repent of his sins and believe on the Saviour (Acts 20:21). But because of man's bondage in sin he is both unwilling and unable to do that, left to himself. In order for people to receive the gospel, certain things must therefore happen.

1. Because man's mind is naturally darkened, he needs to have his understanding enlightened in order that he may appreciate the gospel (2 Corinthians 4:4-6; Acts 26:18; Matthew 16:16-17).
2. Because man's will is enslaved, he needs to be set free and given power to turn to the Lord. He has no power in himself to turn (Acts 11:18; 26:18).

   We speak of man's will being enslaved, but we must realize that this, of necessity, means that his rejection of God is wilful. He is not held captive *against* his will, for it is *his will* that is set against God.
3. Because man's affections are corrupted, a change must occur for him to be brought to love the Lord. But he cannot change himself (Jeremiah 13:23; John 3:5-6).

How can there be any hope?

Does all seem black and hopeless? Left to ourselves it is. But do not despair. Read on!

Read through Mark 10:17-31. Here we see someone who rejects Christ. Why?

____

____

How does this tie up with what we have learned in this lesson?

____

____

Look at verses 24-26. Can a camel go through the eye of a needle? How easy is it for sinners to get themselves saved?

Look at verse 27. How does Jesus sum up man's ability to enter salvation?

But there is hope. Look again at verse 27. Where does Jesus locate the only hope for sinners?

God's initiative and power alone can rescue a sinner.

Read through Ephesians 2:1-10. To whom does this passage ascribe the work of salvation? See particularly verses 4, 6 and 10.

What phraseology does this passage use concerning what happens to someone who becomes saved? Compare verse 1 and verses 4-5.

Our salvation is all of God and all of grace. Look up the following references, which teach that this is the case:

Ephesians 1:4-5; 1 Peter 1:2-3.

Man's inability to help himself or turn to God shows the need for God, out of pure grace and love, to act on his behalf. But how does this work? We must begin to look at that in our next study.

Conclusion

As you reflect on this study, what is the place of prayer in the work of preaching and evangelism?

What have you learned from this study that makes you want to humble yourself before God?

STUDY 6
ELECTION AND PREDESTINATION

You will find it helpful to read through Ephesians 1:1-14 before tackling this study.

ELECTION and PREDESTINATION are not words dreamed up by theologians. They are related biblical words which carry slightly different emphases.

To elect means to make a choice. 'This refers to that work of God's grace whereby he chooses individuals and groups for a purpose or destiny in accordance with his will' (Bruce Milne).

Read 1 Peter 1:1-2. What is the basis of God's choosing, according to verse 2?

___

From these verses how are the three Persons of the Trinity involved in our salvation? Who does what?

___

___

___

To predestinate emphasizes the goal, the end in view, the destination of those who have been chosen.

Read Ephesians 1:5. What is the basis of God's choice, according to this verse?

___

What is the goal of this choice?

___

___

The doctrine of election

The Greek verb for electing is *eklegomai*. It is used both of God's and of Christ's choosing actions. The preposition 'ek' in the verb shows that originally the word indicated 'choosing out of'. Out of all of fallen mankind God has chosen a people for himself.

Read again Ephesians 1:3-14. Write out Ephesians 1:4.

____

____

1. WHICH PERSON OF THE GODHEAD IS ATTRIBUTED WITH CHOOSING US?

   ____

2. WHO OR WHAT DID GOD CHOOSE?

   Paul's answer, in writing to the Christians in Ephesus, is that God chose 'us'. Look at verses 4 and 11. Christians are spoken of as God's elect. Read Mark 13:20 and Colossians 3:12. Note how the history of the world is affected by God's concern for his elect.

3. HOW HAS GOD CHOSEN THEM?

   He has chosen them 'in Christ'. See Ephesians 1:4.

   In Scripture the Lord Jesus Christ is spoken of as the first great chosen One, the head of God's elect.

   Read Isaiah 42:1-3. Who, according to Matthew 12:15-21, is 'my servant' referred to by Isaiah?

   ____

   Read 1 Peter 1:20. Who is the 'he' of this verse and who are the 'you' (implied in 'for your sake')?

   ____

   ____

   Election must never be isolated from Jesus Christ. The elect are saved only through Christ's atoning work on the cross (Ephesians 1:7). All spiritual blessings come to Christians through Christ (Ephesians 1:3). 'In Christ' is one of Paul's favourite expressions.

4. WHEN DID GOD MAKE THIS CHOICE?

   God is working now in the world according to a plan he has already decided upon. He chose us 'before the creation of the world' (Ephesians 1:4). Note that it was *not* a matter of God revising his plans after the events of Genesis 3!

5. WHAT EFFECTS DOES GOD'S CHOICE HAVE ON THOSE CHOSEN?

   It causes them to come to Christ, to be adopted into God's family, to be forgiven and counted blameless in God's sight through the work of Christ, and to live holy lives (Ephesians 1:4-5).

Those whom God chooses, choose God.

Read Romans 8:29-30. What are the consequences of election, according to these verses?

6. WHAT IS THE BASIS ON WHICH GOD MADE HIS CHOICE?

This act of choosing is not based on, nor is it a response to, anything done by those chosen. Read again Romans 8:29. What does this verse say is the reason for God's choosing?

What does Romans 9:11-12 tell us is *not* the basis of God's choosing?

See also 2 Timothy 1:9.

God's choice of people is not based on anything in them. (See also Deuteronomy 7:7-8 and 9:4-6.) In this sense election is 'unconditional'.

Scripture does not teach that God foresees who will believe on Christ and *then* chooses them. The New Testament does not use the word 'foresee' but the word 'foreknow'. He foreknows, not people's actions, but the people themselves (Romans 8:29). For God to foreknow people is for God to set his love upon them, for no reason in them, from before the beginning of time.

The grace of God is absolutely free. If the choice of God is not conditioned in any way by anything in those he chooses, what answer can we give to those who might say, 'I can never be saved, because I am not the kind of person God chooses'?

7. WHAT IS THE ULTIMATE PURPOSE OF GOD IN CHOOSING US?

In accordance with what we saw in the second study, it is for God's own glory (Ephesians 1:6).

We have the marvellous privilege, if we are Christians, of being those through whom the living God has chosen to display how wonderful he is.

That our election is for God's glory is as it should be. He is God and it would be wrong for our election to have any other end exclusively in view (Romans 11:36).

Some objections to consider

To be told that our position is such that we can do nothing to save ourselves and that our rescue depends entirely on the sovereign God and his electing purposes is a very humbling and sobering thought. Thus people often raise objections to the Bible's teaching on election and predestination:

1. 'JESUS TAUGHT A SIMPLE GOSPEL, PAUL COMPLICATED IT WITH ELECTION'

Some people try to play off Paul against the Lord Jesus Christ, and give the impression that the Lord Jesus did not teach election. But apart from the great error implicit in this idea (setting one part of the Bible against another), the charge itself is simply not true. Paul is not the only New Testament writer who teaches election (see 1 Peter 1:2; 2 Peter 1:10; 2 John 1, 13). In fact the Lord Jesus speaks frequently of election in the Gospels. Look up some of the things he said: Matthew 22:14; John 5:21; 6:37, 39, 65; 17:6.

2. 'ELECTION MAKES GOD SEEM UNJUST'

This is an understandable objection which we must answer sensitively. The Bible clearly teaches predestination. But, as we have seen in Study 3, the relationship between God's sovereignty and human choice and responsibility is a great mystery, and although election may *appear* to make God unjust, this is not so (Deuteronomy 32:4).

Read Romans 9:19-21. How does Paul respond to the accusation that God is unfair in his election of some and not of others?

____

____

____

____

We may have the question in our minds, 'Why didn't God elect the whole human race and save everybody; surely this would be more just?' The following words written by B. B. Warfield are illuminating: 'The physician who, having the power to treat and cure all his patients, arbitrarily discriminates between them and contents himself with ministering to some of them only, would justly incur the reprobation of men. But may not the judge, having the power to release all his criminals, be held back by higher considerations from releasing them all? It may be inexplicable why a physician in the case supposed should not relieve all; while the wonder may be in the case of the judge rather how he can release any. The love of God is in its exercise necessarily under the control of his righteousness; and to plead that love has suffered an eclipse because he does not do all that he has the bare power to do, is in effect to deny to him a moral nature. The real solution to the puzzle that is raised with respect to the distribution of divine grace is, then, not to be sought along the lines either of the denial of the omnipotence of God's grace with the Arminians, or of the denial of the reality of his reprobation with our neo-universalists, but in the affirmation of his righteousness. The old answer is after all the only sufficient one: God in his love saves as many of the guilty race of man as he can get the consent of his whole nature to save. Being God and all that God is, he will not permit even his ineffable love to betray him into any action which is not right. And it is therefore that we praise him and trust him and love him. For he is not part God, a God here and there, with some but not all the attributes which belong to true God: he is God altogether, God through and through, all that God is and all that God ought to be.' [7]

3. 'ELECTION DENIES HUMAN FREE WILL'

This is an age-old puzzle which we considered in Study 3. People commonly speak of free will, but the Bible does not speak of free will in the commonly accepted sense. As we saw in Study 3, our relationship to the sovereign God is more complex than we can comprehend. He is sovereign and at the same time we are responsible.

In fact, when the Bible speaks of man's will in the context of salvation, it emphasizes its *bondage*, not its freedom. Our moral and spiritual slavery is one of the principal things from which we need to be saved.

Look up John 8:34 and 2 Timothy 2:25-26. To what is man in bondage?

God needs to act first and this is what he has done in his love.

Election and predestination in the church confessions

Election and predestination are taught in the great confessions of faith of the church.

ARTICLE 17 OF THE THIRTY-NINE ARTICLES

'Predestination to Life is the everlasting purpose of God, whereby . . . he hath continually decreed . . . to deliver from curse and damnation those whom he hath chosen in Christ . . . and to bring them by Christ to everlasting salvation.'

THE WESTMINSTER CONFESSION OF FAITH

'Those . . . predestinated unto life, God . . . hath chosen in Christ unto everlasting glory, out of his mere free grace and love, without any foresight of faith or good works.'

THE BAPTIST CONFESSION OF FAITH, 1689

'God hath predestined (or foreordained) certain men . . . to eternal life through Jesus Christ.'

The New Testament use of this doctrine

It is *never* used in Scripture to discourage any sincere seeker after Christ.

The New Testament uses this doctrine primarily for the encouragement of Christians. It assures us that it is not simply that we have chosen Christ, but rather that God has chosen us. Our salvation begins with God, and what God begins he always finishes; nothing ever thwarts his ultimate purposes. 'Will I be saved in the end?' 'Will I be able to keep on with the Christian life?' 'Is it really *me* that God loves?' This truth answers such questions with an all-conquering *yes!*

Read through Romans 8:28-31 and Ephesians 1:1-14 and write a list of the benefits that are yours as a Christian through election and the sovereign purposes of God.

____

____

____

____

The truth about predestination should fix our minds on our destiny, which is holiness to the glory of God. Thus we should live our lives now in the light of that destination.

We are chosen to be happy in heaven and holy on earth.

Conclusion

It would be of great encouragement to you if you were to learn by heart Ephesians 1:4-6.

A simple method of doing this is to

> Read the verses out loud three times,
> Write the verses on paper three times,
> Recite the verses without looking three times,
> Review the verses three times a day for a week.

STUDY 7
WHY DID JESUS CHRIST DIE?

The apostle Paul wrote of his personal outlook on life: 'God forbid that I should glory, save in the *cross* of our Lord Jesus Christ' (Galatians 6:14). With regard to his gospel preaching he wrote: 'I resolved to know nothing while I was with you except Jesus Christ and him *crucified*' (1 Corinthians 2:2). The great purpose of the church communion service or Lord's supper, instituted by the Lord Jesus on the night he was betrayed, is that we should remember 'the Lord's *death* until he comes' (1 Corinthians 11:26).

The cross is central to Christianity. All Christians know that the death of Jesus on the cross was 'for our sins', but what does that actually mean? How does what happened at Calvary bring about our forgiveness? We consider these things in this lesson.

How can a holy God grant forgiveness?

Read through Isaiah 6:1-4. Which characteristic of God is the focus of attention in these verses?

Read Exodus 3:5 and 19:10-13. What was it about the Lord that meant that people had to take the utmost care in their approach to him?

Look at Job 42:5-6 and Luke 5:8. What was it about the Lord that caused Job and Peter to feel so wretched and unclean in his presence?

The holiness of God, his impeccable and beautiful moral purity, is in many ways the dominant attribute of God. And for that reason forgiving sins is not a simple task for God. It is a great mistake for us to think that it is.

Why do you think it is in many ways easier for us to forgive our fellow-men than it is for God to forgive people? See Ephesians 4:32; Matthew 18:32-33.

But unlike us, God is holy and indeed his holy character is the ground upon which all moral values in the universe depend. For God to do or be seen to agree to anything unholy would be to un-God himself and throw the whole of creation into chaos.

The difficulty for God is how to forgive people without compromising his holy character. If he merely overlooks evil, it is as good as saying that evil does not matter. That would make him no better than the devil. As the holy God, his righteousness — that is, his opposition to all evil — must be demonstrated. How could God forgive people and still be on the side of righteousness and be seen to be so? This was, as it were, the 'obstacle' to be overcome as he contemplated saving us.

How can God show his righteousness?

1. GOD THE JUDGE

   The first and most obvious way for God to demonstrate his righteousness is by his role as the Judge of all the earth. This means at least two things.

   (a) God declares and publicly backs his holy law, summarized, for example, in the Ten Commandments (Exodus 20:1-17) or in another way in 1 Corinthians 13:1-8.

   How can these two passages be considered to be equivalent in expressing the moral law? See Romans 13:8-10 for help.

How did the Lord Jesus Christ publicly endorse the moral law of God in his Sermon on the Mount? See Matthew 5:17-18.

(b) God as Judge executes penalties upon those who break his holy law.

Read Ezekiel 18:4; Romans 2:8-9; 6:23. What is the penalty for sin?

How did Jesus speak of the penalty for sin in the Sermon on the Mount? See Matthew 5:21-22, 27-30.

However, this demonstration of God's righteousness, through his assuming the role of the Judge, results in the condemnation of the whole human race (Romans 3:20, 23).

If people are to be saved, some other way must be found.

2. CHRIST THE SAVIOUR

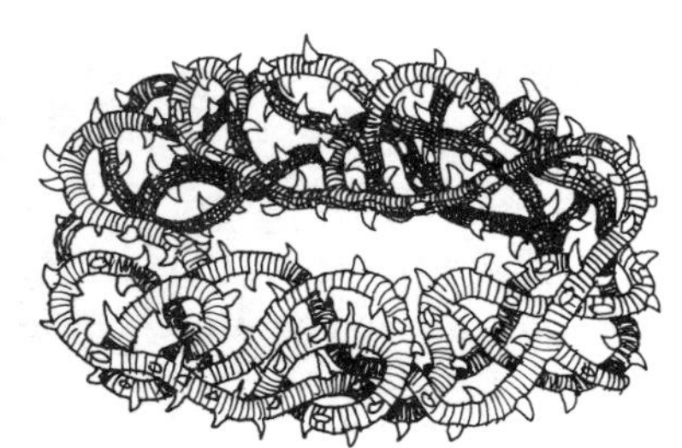

Is it possible for the righteousness and holiness of God to be asserted in some other way so that people can be saved and so that God's justice actually acquits people rather than condemns them? It would seem impossible.

However, the good news of the gospel is that through the coming of the Lord Jesus Christ, it *is* possible. God sent his Son into the world as a man among men; he lived a spotless and holy life wholly pleasing to God, and through his death on the cross all who believe are counted righteous in God's sight and saved.

Read through Romans 3:21-26.

How do we *not* achieve righteousness in God's sight? (verse 21).

How does the gift of righteousness become ours? (verse 22)

Where does this righteousness spring from? (verse 24)

It *is* possible for God to be righteous and holy and at the same time acquit and pardon sinners! See Romans 3:25-26 for the evidence.

This alternative way of God's demonstrating his righteousness finds its focus in his Son, Jesus Christ.

The central purpose of the cross: subjective or objective?

Some people want to treat the death of Christ as if its only design was to have some subjective effect upon us.

There is the *moral influence* theory. This holds that Christ's death was a great demonstration of God's love towards us which moves us to change our minds about God and so love him.

Then there is the *moral example* theory. This holds that the death of Christ was an illustration of perfect obedience to God and as such it shows us how we ought to live. It convicts us of our selfishness and sin so that we decide to reform our lives.

Then there is the *mystical union* theory. In the cross we see God suffering in the same way as we suffer in our fallen world, so we are led to faith, feeling that God is with us amidst the struggles of our lives.

Each of these theories has an element of truth in it, but they all miss the central purpose of the cross.

Look at Psalm 51:1-12. Note the psalmist's concern with his guilt before God and the deep-rootedness of sin in his life. How do such theories of the cross fail to address these vital matters?

These theories speak about the cross changing us and our attitudes, but the New Testament speaks of the cross making a difference not, first of all, to us, but to God.

It was the objective demonstration and satisfaction of his righteousness (Romans 3:25-26; Mark 10:45).

At the cross God showed his abhorrence of, and total opposition to, sin. At the cross he meted out just punishment for sin, just as he does when he punishes sinners in hell, but in a different way. Thus God's righteousness was demonstrated and his justice satisfied.

Jesus Christ our substitute

There are many aspects to the cross, but its central significance is as a substitutionary sacrifice, that is, Jesus died in the sinner's place as a sacrifice to pay the penalty of sin.

The Old Testament prophet Isaiah predicted the sufferings of the Lord Jesus Christ as our Saviour (see Acts 8:32-35).

Read through Isaiah 52:13 to 53:12.

This passage of Scripture, which speaks prophetically of our Lord Jesus Christ, is full of the language of substitution.

'. . . as a sheep before her shearers is silent, so he did not open his mouth.'

Whose sorrows did Christ carry? (verse 4)

____

For what was Christ pierced and crushed? (verse 5)

____

How is it that we have peace and healing? (verse 5)

____

What was it that the LORD laid upon Christ? (verse 6)

____

So it is that the Christian can rightly speak in terms of Christ being our substitute, dying in our place (Isaiah 53:8).

There are three important words which the New Testament uses to describe what was achieved at the cross when Jesus died in our place.

1. REDEMPTION (Romans 3:24; Colossians 1:14)

   The background to this term is the slave-market where a ransom was paid to a slave-owner in place of the slave, in order to effect the slave's release.

Likewise, Christ died in our place to release us from the deserts of sin. What did Jesus say about himself in Mark 10:45?

____

____

2. PROPITIATION (Romans 3:25; 1 John 2:2)

   This word is translated as 'atoning sacrifice' in the NIV. When someone is propitiated, he has been appeased, his anger has been averted and turned away. Christ dying in our place took the full force of God's anger against sin for us and God is angry no more with us. What does this word tell us about the nature of sin?

   ____

   ____

3. RECONCILIATION (Romans 5:10; 2 Corinthians 5:20-21)

   When an enemy becomes our friend, he has been reconciled. Through Christ's substitutionary death, we have been reconciled to God.

Behind all this there is an extensive Old Testament background. God set up the cross in the context of Old Testament Judaism in order to show how Christ's death should be interpreted. Some of these Old Testament pictures are:

1. ISAAC'S RAM (Genesis 22:1-19)

   Look particularly at Genesis 22:13. Write out the expression which speaks of the ram being offered as a substitute.

   ____

   Who provided the sacrifice? (verse 8)

2. THE PASSOVER (Exodus 12:1-28)

   How could God be faithful to his promises to Israel when they were as much sinners as the Egyptians? (verses 12-13) The day after the angel of death passed through the land in judgment, there was a dead son in every Egyptian home; while in every Israelite home there was a dead lamb. Each eldest son in Israel could say that the angel of death had passed over him because a 'passover lamb' had died for him. How is this a picture of our salvation? (1 Corinthians 5:7)

   ____

   ____

   ____

3. THE DAY OF ATONEMENT (Leviticus 16:1-34)

In the darkness of the Holy of Holies, where only God could see, the blood was sprinkled to make atonement for the sins of God's people. Christ's death satisfies God's justice (Hebrews 9:24-28).

It was against this Old Testament background that John the Baptist was able triumphantly to announce concerning Jesus, 'Look, the Lamb of God, who takes away the sin of the world!' (John 1:29).

His holy fingers formed the bough
Where grew the thorns that crowned his brow.
The nails that pierced his hands were mined
In secret places he designed.

He made the forests whence there sprung
The tree on which his body hung.
He died upon a cross of wood,
Yet made the hill upon which it stood.

The sun which hid from him its face,
By his decree was poised in space.
The sky which darkened o'er his head,
By him above the earth was spread.

The spear that spilt his precious blood
Was tempered in the fires of God.
The grave in which his form was laid
Was hewn in rocks his hands had made.

F. W. Pitt [8]

How do these verses, which reflect the teaching of Scripture, answer the question, 'How could the death of one person bring about eternal salvation for so many people?'

Conclusion

Reflect on what you have learned in this study and use it in prayer, worship and thanksgiving to the Lord.

STUDY 8
FOR WHOM DID CHRIST DIE?

We saw in the previous study that the New Testament teaches that, on the cross, as a substitutionary sacrifice, the Lord Jesus:

— actually redeemed people from the consequences of their sin (Galatians 3:13);

— actually turned away the just anger of God against them (Romans 3:25; 1 John 4:10);

— actually reconciled people to God (Romans 5:10).

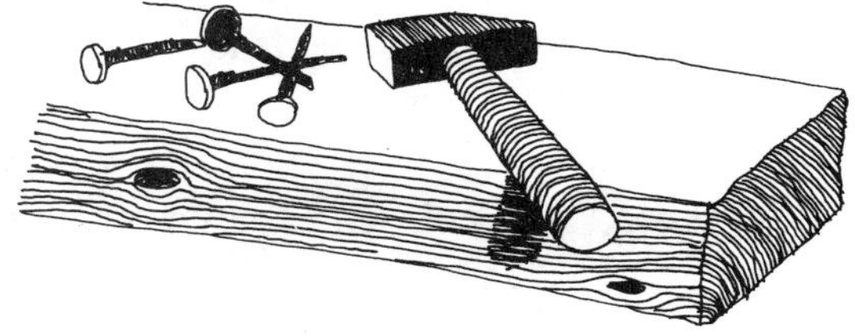

For whom did Christ do this?

There are three possible answers.

1. FOR ALL THE SINS OF ALL MEN

   This is universalism, which holds that Christ has paid the penalty for everyone's sins, and hence all men are saved.

   There is certainly a universal *relevance* in the death of Christ, as we shall see later, but it is clear from the Bible that hell is not an empty threat on God's part. (In fact an empty threat would be dishonest and contrary to God's nature.) How do we know that not everybody will be saved? Look up Matthew 13:41-42 and Revelation 20:15.

   ____

   ____

2. FOR SOME OF THE SINS OF ALL MEN

   But if Christ has not cleared the total debt of an individual's sin it means that person's salvation depends at least in part on his own ability to atone for sin and satisfy God's holy standards.

   It is clear that the Holy Spirit does enable believers to overcome the power of sin in their lives, but the Bible is opposed to any thought of human merit contributing in the slightest to the work of salvation itself.

   Read Romans 3:27 and Ephesians 2:8-10. Why are 'works' which we have done excluded, according to these verses?

   ____

   ____

   See also 2 Timothy 1:9.

3. FOR ALL THE SINS OF SOME MEN

This means that certain people are definitely saved. There is a definite atonement (sometimes this is spoken of as 'limited atonement' or 'particular redemption' — redemption of particular people). God intended to save a definite company of people out of the fallen human race. This is consistent with what we have seen in the doctrine of election. At the cross Christ saved all who believe, the elect of God.

Many New Testament verses point to the truth of particular redemption. For example, look up the following verses:

Matthew 1:21. Whom will Jesus save?

John 6:37-40. Who will have eternal life?

John 10:14-16, 26-28. For whom did the Good Shepherd die?

Acts 20:28. Whom did the Lord purchase and at what price?

Hebrews 10:14. Whom has Christ made perfect in God's sight by his sacrifice?

You might like to look up these verses too: John 15:13-14; Romans 8:31-34; 1 Corinthians 8:11; Ephesians 5:25-27; 1 John 4:10-11.

The New Testament teaches that, on the cross, Jesus did not simply make salvation possible, but actually saved all those who believe.

The debt is paid, once and for all.

Commenting on 2 Corinthians 5:21 the Puritan theologian, John Owen, writes: 'What is it, then? "He made him to be sin who knew no sin"? Why, clearly, by dispensation and consent, he [God] laid that to his [Christ's] charge whereof he was not guilty. He charged upon him and imputed unto him all the sins of all the elect, and proceeded against him accordingly. He stood as our surety, really charged with the whole debt, and was to pay the utmost farthing, as a surety is to do if it is required of him; though he borrow not the money, nor have one penny of that which is in the obligation, yet if he be sued to an execution, he must pay all. The Lord Christ (if I may so say) was sued by his Father's justice unto an execution, in answer whereunto he underwent all that was due to sin; which we proved before to be death, wrath, and curse.' [9]

Some objections and clarifications

1. Of course, there are verses in the New Testament which appear to teach that Christ died for 'all' or 'everyone', but we must read these words in context. If you think about it, you will realize that we often use these words in a limited rather than universal sense.

   As examples we consider two passages.

   First look at 2 Corinthians 5:14-15. What distinguishes the 'all' for whom Christ died, according to verse 15?

   Secondly, look at Hebrews 2:9-13. Note the link between 'everyone' (verse 9), 'many sons' (verse 10), 'brothers' (verses 11-12), 'children' (verse 13) and 'their salvation' (verse 10). Now, who are the 'everyone' spoken of in verse 9?

   Often the Bible uses the word 'all' to mean not 'all people everywhere' but all of a particular group of people, and the context makes it clear who this group are (consider John 12:32 and note verses 38-40).

   Similarly, the word 'world' needs to be read in context. A good example is John 4:42. This verse speaks of Christ as 'the Saviour of the world'. Does that mean that everyone throughout all history and in all places will be saved? No, this verse is not teaching universalism; that would be in contradiction to the rest of the Bible. But the verse is teaching that Christ is the one and only Saviour for anyone anywhere in this world; salvation will be found in no one else.

2. But we need to see that the death of Christ has a universal relevance. There are two aspects to this:

   (a) Jesus died for all in the sense that he died in order that there should be a gospel of grace which is open to all and freely offered to all. Read Luke 24:46-47 and the most famous verse in the Bible, John 3:16.

To whom is the forgiveness of sins to be proclaimed?

For whom is it effective?

The gospel is to be offered to all, and it is man's own responsibility and sin if he refuses God's saving offer. We touch here again upon the mystery surrounding God's sovereignty in election and man's responsibility. We may imagine that the doctrine of election would preclude a free offer of forgiveness to all the world. But biblically this is not so. The biblical gospel call is not 'Are you one of the elect? If you are you may believe and be saved'. It is 'Believe on the Lord Jesus Christ — and if you do you are one of God's elect'. Christ's death was for all in that all who believe will be saved by him.

(b) There is another universal aspect to the death of Christ in that his death purchased the day of grace for all men. For God to allow the history of the world to continue after the Fall was to allow sin to continue and develop when he could have put an immediate stop to it by destroying the world. But God wanted history to continue in order that his saving purposes might be worked out. The death of Christ purchased that postponement of judgment at the bar of God.

So it is that some verses in the Scriptures speak of Christ dying for those who are lost. For example, 2 Peter 2:1 speaks of godless false teachers being 'bought' by the Lord.

> *The Puritan commentator, Matthew Poole, writes on 2 Peter 2:1: 'Christ bought or redeemed them ... in that by his death he purchased the continuance of their lives, and the staying of their execution, and rescued them from that present [imminent] destruction which, without Christ's interposition, had seized on them, as it had likewise on the whole visible creation immediately upon the apostasy of mankind.'* [10]

It is this delaying of judgment which is one of the things at the back of Paul's mind in Acts 17:30 and Romans 3:25.

In the light of what we have just seen, consider the following verses and say how you think they should be understood.

1 Timothy 4:10

____

____

____

____

1 Timothy 2:6

____

____

____

____

1 John 2:2

____

____

____

____

Why is this doctrine of particular redemption important?

1. It is important because it secures the fact that *Jesus saves us*. On the cross the work of redemption was completed and finished once and for all (John 19:30; Hebrews 9:26). The Lord Jesus Christ has done *everything* necessary to save those who believe and thus we can rejoice in our security in Christ.

   At what times in our Christian experience is the thought of a completed salvation of especial comfort to us?

   ____

   ____

   ____

2. It is important because it tells us that we as Christians can say to ourselves, 'Jesus loves *me*'. When he died on the cross Christ was not dying for a mass of nameless individuals. He was dying for his chosen ones. He was bearing *our* sins. The Christian can know that 'Christ was dying for *me*'.

Read Galatians 2:20. What effect did the realization of this have on the apostle Paul?

___

___

___

3. It is important because it secures to the believer the truth of Romans 8:32-39. If God gave his Son to die for us particularly and effectually, we can be assured that he will not withhold any other good from us.

   What is the greatest gift God has given us?

   ___

   ___

   Since he has given us this, the most costly and greatest gift, he is hardly likely to withhold lesser things from us, is he? What an encouragement that is to our faith!

Conclusion

Read the following paragraph and meditate on Christ's death on the cross in the light of it.

> *The 19th-century American preacher, Gardiner Spring, writes: 'It is no easy matter to persuade a man who is fallen by his iniquity and who is deeply sensible that he deserves to perish, that there is a refuge from coming wrath. He may discover some probabilities of pardon; he may indulge some flickering hopes: but these occasional flashes from the dark sky do not compose his fears. Nor are they tranquilized, nor can they be, until the storm has spent its fury and he sees the rainbow painted in the cloud. Such a man, more especially if, in the days of his thoughtlessness and vanity, he has had loose notions of the Divine justice, and presumptuous expectations from the Divine mercy, is much more disposed to believe that God cannot be just and pardon, than that he would be unjust to punish and destroy. To stand on a strong and immovable foundation, he must be placed in the position where justice has no claims upon him, and where the penalty of the law is satisfied, because all his sins are atoned for. This is the only solace for the wounded conscience; it is the refuge the sinner needs; it is the refuge furnished by the cross, because the cross furnishes the only effective propitiation for his sins.'* [11]

STUDY 9
HOW GOD'S GRACE COMES TO US

'What must I do to be saved?' That was the question the Philippian jailer asked Paul and Silas (Acts 16:30). He had been made desperately aware of the frailty of his life as an earthquake shook the foundations of his prison. Having seen what Jesus has done for sinners, and realizing the frailty of our own lives, it is a question which we all ought to ask ourselves.

God's grace provides forgiveness for sinners through the death of Christ. It brings us to know God and be accepted by him, because we are redeemed at Christ's expense. But how does that grace — that forgiveness, that spiritual life — come to take effect in our lives?

Personal faith

1. GOD DEALS WITH US AS INDIVIDUALS

The first thing Scripture insists on is that salvation is personal. To be born in a 'Christian' country where we can easily hear the gospel, to be part of a Christian family where the Bible is read, to go along each Sunday with the crowd to church — these are all good things, but they are insufficient to save us. For forgiveness and spiritual life to be ours, God must deal with us as individuals.

How did Jesus emphasize this to the religious teacher, Nicodemus, in John 3:1-8?

____

____

2. ONLY ONE MEDIATOR

Secondly, we may ask, 'How is it possible for people to have dealings with God at a personal, individual level? Do we not need someone to act as a go-between?' Roman Catholic dogma has always seen the church as a kind of middle-man between God and sinners, and conceives of grace as a sort of spiritual substance mediated through the priests and the sacraments to the individual. Thus the traditional Catholic view has been that there can be no salvation outside the Roman Catholic Church.

But the Bible teaches that Jesus Christ is our priest, and he is the one and only intermediary between God and men. So, knowing the promises of God in the gospel, we are invited to go directly to God through Christ.

Write out 1 Timothy 2:5

Write out 1 John 2:1

3. FAITH ALONE

Look up Acts 16:30-31. What was the apostle Paul's answer to the man who asked the question, 'What must I do to be saved?'

Velkommen
NORWEGIAN

Welkom
AFRIKAANS-DUTCH

Bienvenue
FRENCH

Benvenuto
ITALIAN

Välkomna
SWEDISH

Bienvenido
SPANISH

ようこそ
JAPANESE

Bem-vindo
PORTUGUESE

歡迎
MANDARIN CHINESE

Willkommen
GERMAN

The good news is of a God who welcomes sinners.

We receive forgiveness and spiritual life from God as the Holy Spirit operates in our hearts to bring us to faith in the Lord Jesus Christ.

Check this by looking up John 3:16; Romans 3:22; 5:1.

The biblical teaching of salvation through faith is a surprise to many people. People tend to think of religion in terms of earning a place in heaven by being good and keeping the rules. Christianity is popularly seen to consist of being law-abiding citizens, living good lives and being kind to our neighbours. But that is to misunderstand and to put the cart before the horse.

The Bible teaches categorically that we are not saved by our good deeds (Romans 3:20). They could never be good enough in the sight of the all-holy God, and we know it. We do not merit salvation. But the wonderful teaching of the gospel is that Christ has merited salvation for us; he has purchased it for his people with his blood. His people are those who have faith in him. We are saved through faith in Christ.*

Once we are saved and know the joy of God's forgiveness, we will want to live so as to please him out of gratitude for his love. However, it is not good deeds, but faith, simple personal trust in Christ, which brings salvation.

In Galatians 2:15-16 Paul says that salvation is by faith alone and not by good works. Read these verses and then try to rewrite them using your own words.

It was Martin Luther's rediscovery of the fact that God gives grace directly into the hands of faith without the mediation of the church and without our deserving it through our 'good works', that led to the great revival of spiritual life, truth and joy known as the Reformation. The sheer delight in realizing that none are too bad or too far gone for Christ to save them as they come to him in faith, swept the continent of Europe and changed the course of history. *Sola fide* ('faith alone') was the war-cry of the Reformation.

* Sometimes in Scripture you will find that the requirement for salvation is spoken of as faith (Acts 16:31), sometimes as repentance (Luke 24:47) and sometimes as repentance and faith (Mark 1:15; Acts 20:21). The reason is that repentance and faith are part and parcel of the same thing; they are two sides of the same coin.

True faith is the turning of the soul in trust towards the Lord. But to turn sincerely to the Lord necessarily involves turning away from sin and self. Thus true faith includes repentance.

True repentance means turning our back on sin with sorrow for the past and practically pursuing what is right and good. But we can pursue what is right and good only as we trust and serve the Lord who is the fountain of all that is right and good. Thus true repentance includes faith.

We receive God's grace through faith alone. Faith is the turning of the soul to take hold on the Lord through faith in Christ and his atoning work which brings salvation to the individual.

How do we come to believe?

Some people have taught that all men have by nature the ability to believe in Christ if they choose. This idea is called Pelagianism after Pelagius, a British monk, who propounded it during the 4th and 5th centuries.

But read 2 Corinthians 4:4. How does this verse show that Pelagianism is wrong?

____

____

____

Others acknowledge the spiritual blindness and powerlessness of sinners but say that God comes and gives to all men sufficient grace to rise, as it were, above the fetters of sin, and at that point they must of themselves alone make a free choice to believe on the Saviour. This belief is called Arminianism, after Arminius, a Dutch theologian who lived during the 17th century.

But read Matthew 11:25-27. How do these verses show us that Jesus did not have an Arminian view of how people come to repent and believe?

____

____

____

Yet others hold that the elect of God are so acted upon by the Holy Spirit, who changes their nature, that they are made willing to trust in Christ and do so. Naturally, because of our fallen condition, all men resist the call of the gospel, but by this 'irresistible grace' or 'effectual calling' of God, the mind, heart and will of man are changed so that he is happy to trust the Saviour. Historically this view is known as Calvinism, after the 16th-century French Reformer.

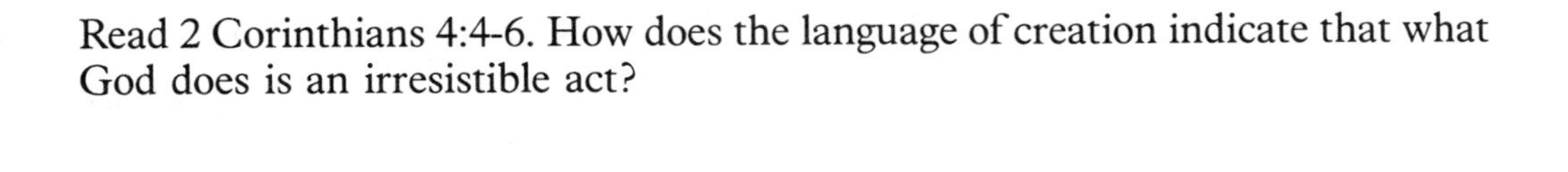

Read 2 Corinthians 4:4-6. How does the language of creation indicate that what God does is an irresistible act?

While the third view may not be without some difficulties for us philosophically, the first and second are fraught with great problems in the light of Scripture.

These views are such that salvation is, at least partly, seen as man's doing. Everything is made to hang on man's unaided choice of Christ. This is contrary to the teaching of Scripture that our salvation is all of God from first to last.

These views imply that Christ's death on the cross was a momentous gamble on God's part, as it had no assured outcome. Christ could have died without anyone choosing to be saved!

> *B. B. Warfield writes: 'We hear ringing up and down the land the passionate proclamation of what its adherents love to call a "whosoever will gospel". It is no doubt the universality of the gospel offer which is intended to be emphasized. But do we not shoot beyond the mark when we seem to hang salvation purely on the human will? And should we not stop to consider that, if we seem to open salvation to* "whosoever *will" on the one hand, on the other we open it only to "whosoever* will"? *And who, in this world of death and sin, I do not say merely will, but can, will the good? Is it not forever true that grapes are not gathered from thorns, nor figs from thistles; that it is only the good tree which brings forth good fruit while the evil tree brings forth always and everywhere only evil fruit? It is not only Hannah More's Black Giles the Poacher who may haply "find it difficult to repent when he will". It is useless to talk of salvation being for "whosoever will" in a world of universal "won't". Here is the real point of difficulty: how, where, can we obtain* the will? *Let others rejoice in a "whosoever will gospel": for the sinner who knows himself to be a sinner, and knows what it is to be a sinner, only a "God will" gospel will suffice. If the gospel is to be committed to the dead wills of sinful men, and there is nothing above and beyond, who then can be saved?'* [12]

The key truths and Scripture passages

First of all notice how this truth of effectual calling again fits in with all we have seen so far. If men are spiritually blind and dead and unable to save themselves because of sin, if God in his grace has purposed to save them, and if Christ has died in order to procure that salvation, it follows logically that God must also provide the means of calling them into the benefits of the salvation he has constructed for them. God effectually calls the elect into spiritual life and forgiveness.

Secondly, not only is this logical, but it is the teaching of the Scriptures.

1. The work of the Holy Spirit is absolutely necessary for us to be able to see the truth of the gospel and believe (John 3:3; 1 Corinthians 2:12).

2. Faith is not simply our response to Christ: it is a gift to us from God (Matthew 16:17; Ephesians 2:8; Philippians 1:29).

   Consider the teaching of Ephesians 2:8. By what are we saved?

   ____

   ____

   How does this grace come to us?

   ____

   ____

   Where does the means of receiving this grace come from?

   ____

   ____

3. Christ himself spoke clearly and uncompromisingly of the irresistibility of God's saving grace. Read these verses: John 6:36-37, 44, 64-65.

   What does Christ say 'no one' can do?

   ____

   ____

   How does verse 37 show us that Jesus knew God's grace to be irresistible?

   ____

   ____

There are three biblical pictures of effectual calling which illustrate these truths.

1. RESURRECTION

   Look at John 5:24-26 and Ephesians 2:1, 5. How do these texts illustrate man's inability to turn to Christ?

   ____

   ____

How do the events of Easter morning give us confidence in God's ability to bring about conversion in people?

---

2. NEW BIRTH

Look at John 3:1-8; 1 Peter 1:3, 23. What contribution does a baby make to giving itself life?

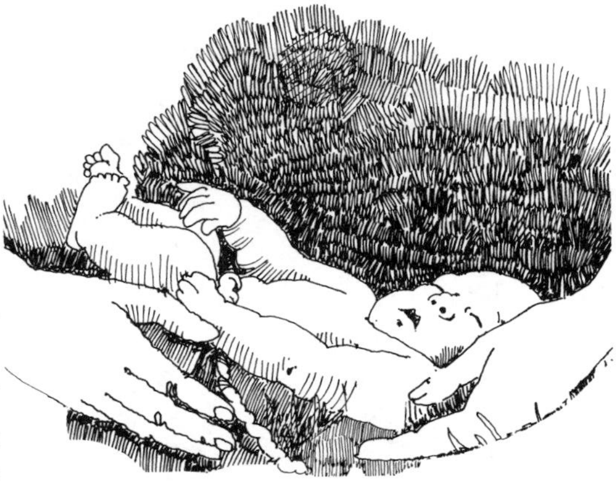

Who has power to bring about the life of a baby? Who alone has power to bring people to conversion and salvation?

---

3. NEW CREATION

Look at 2 Corinthians 4:6; 5:17. Did the world make itself or did God create it? Who ultimately makes us Christians?

Read Ephesians 2:10. How do good works fit into God's programme of our salvation?

However, having seen that effectual calling is the work of God, and that without his work people cannot be converted, it would be wrong to infer that therefore we should not exhort people to come to Christ or command them to repent and believe. (Remember Study 3 concerning God's sovereignty and man's responsibility.)

Read Matthew 11:25-30. Our Lord Jesus Christ was happy to hold the truth of God's sovereignty in salvation (verses 25-27) alongside the free offer of the gospel to all who would come (verses 28-30).

B. B. Warfield explains: 'We may point out, therefore, that the doctrine of inability does not affirm that we cannot believe, but only that we cannot believe in our own strength. It affirms only that there is no natural strength within us by which we may attain to belief. But this is far from asserting that on making the effort we shall find it impossible to believe. We may believe, in God's strength. Our case is parallel to the man with the withered hand. He knew he could not stretch it forth: that is the very characteristic of a withered hand — it was impotent. But Christ commanded, and he stretched it forth. So God commands what he wills and gives what he commands. Unable in ourselves we may taste and see that the Lord is gracious.' [13]

Conclusion

In the light of what you have learned in this study, how would you encourage a non-Christian friend who came to you and said he wished he had your faith and would like to believe but cannot?

____

____

____

____

The truths that we have learned cause the Christian to go about evangelism both expectantly and prayerfully. We cannot bring people to faith in Christ, but God can!

C. H. Spurgeon says: 'The cross of Christ is not put up there merely for every man to look at, and then left to chance as to whether men will look or no. There stands the cross free to every soul that lives, but, nevertheless, God has determined that it shall not be neglected. There is a number that no man can number, who shall, by all-constraining grace, be brought to clasp that cross as the hope of their souls. Jesus shall not die in vain, and that because God will make men willing in the day of his power.' [14]

STUDY 10
THE MARKS OF GRACE

'My sheep listen to my voice; I know them, and they follow me' (John 10:27).

How can someone be sure that he has been saved?

When we become Christians we know to some extent the wonderful subjective experience of the Holy Spirit witnessing with our spirit that we are the children of God (Romans 8:16). The Holy Spirit in our hearts assures us of the truth of God's saving promises and causes us to rest in them.

But apart from this subjective experience, there are objective changes in our lives which evidence the fact that we have been saved. Our thinking and and our desires and our behaviour begin to change out of love for Christ, and such changes point to our having the Lord in our lives. A saved person begins to show these marks of grace.

This process of change does not smother or suffocate our own individuality. It actually brings us great blessing as we are renewed and become the people God intended us to be.

For what great change has God predestinated us? (Romans 8:29)

____

____

According to 2 Corinthians 3:18, what will happen to us as we live a life of looking to Christ by faith?

____

____

Christ is the holy Son of God, and when we become Christians our lives begin to change, so that we too begin to live holy lives like him. This process of change will vary to some extent from Christian to Christian, but it should be plain that the process of changing to become more like Christ has begun and is continuing. That we grow and change into the likeness of God's Son is the sign that we are spiritually alive.

Another way of looking at this is to say that we become Christians through repentance and faith, and repentance and faith imply change. We will never be perfect until we reach heaven, and so our Christian walk in this world is a continuous walk of repentance and faith (Matthew 6:12).

Write out Paul's instructions for Christian living in Colossians 2:6-7.

____

____

____

Is there any difference between the way we start as Christians and the way we go on?

____

The theologian J. I. Packer has a most helpful comment concerning the nature of repentance. He says: 'Repentance means turning from as much as you know of your sin to give as much as you know of yourself to as much as you know of your God, and as our knowledge grows at these three points so our practice of repentance has to be enlarged.' [15] *Thus continuing change and repentance are an inevitable part of a growing relationship with God.*

The marks of grace in the New Testament

How does the New Testament describe the marks of grace? Different preachers and writers in the New Testament approach the subject of the marks of grace in people's lives from different perspectives. They are all speaking about the same thing, but they have different ways of putting it and different emphases. Let us try to get an overview of the main ways in which the grace of God comes to be seen in people's lives.

THE LORD JESUS CHRIST: THE NARROW WAY

In his Sermon on the Mount, the Lord Jesus Christ describes the attitudes and life-style of those who belong to his kingdom. As he concludes his message he encourages people to become Christians with the words: 'Enter through the narrow gate. For wide is the gate and broad is the road that leads to destruction, and many enter through it. But small is the gate and narrow the road that leads to life, and only a few find it' (Matthew 7:13-14).

The Lord Jesus does not want people to be deceived by thinking they are saved when they are not. He characterizes true Christian living as a difficult, narrow way. God's grace is shown in people's lives as they walk the narrow way. But what is the narrow way? Christ has already spelled it out in his sermon.

Here are seven characteristics of the narrow way found in the Sermon on the Mount.

1. The Christian is one who knows his own spiritual bankruptcy but finds all spiritual riches in the Lord. His motivation in life is love for God who so loved him.

   Read Matthew 5:3-10. How do these verses speak of a Christian as one who has changed radically?

   ____

   ____

   ____

   How does this outlook on life contrast with modern ideas of needing to have faith in oneself and self-confidence?

   ____

   ____

2. The Christian is one who experiences varying degrees of social rejection because of his faith.

   We are not to be unfriendly or odd people. We are to be full of love towards others. But even so the Christian will know antipathy from people in the world (Matthew 5:10-12).

   If the Christian is to be a kind, outgoing person why is it that he meets with rejection?

   ____

   ____

3. The Christian is one who lives a life of open witness to Christ (Matthew 5:14-16).

   It is not easy to live openly for Christ. But why is a witnessing faith the only true faith? (See Matthew 10:32-33.)

   ____

   ____

4. The Christian is one who lives a life of daily self-denial and conflict with sin. He may not always win this battle, but he always seeks to fight in it.

How does Christ picture the urgency with which we should fight sin, in Matthew 5:29-30?

5. The Christian is one who is called to a life of forgiveness and sensitive, self-giving love (Matthew 5:38-48). Only as he has known God's love and forgiveness will he be able to love others.

   Why is it hard to love as Christ commands us? How should such love mark us off from others? (verses 46-47)

6. The Christian is one who must choose to reject the world and its values.

   Worldly religion looks for the applause of people, but the Christian must reject that and look only to pleasing God (Matthew 6:1).

   'What was our life's direction before we became Christian? Upward mobility! What is our life's direction after we become Christian? Upward mobility — except God is there to help us become more successful.' What is wrong with this statement, according to Matthew 6:19-24?

7. While as Christians we use our five senses, we are to live by faith and not by sight: we are called to a heaven we have never seen, by a Saviour whom we have never seen, through obedience to his commands.

   Who is the wise man, according to Matthew 7:24-27?

The mark that we have truly received the grace of God and are subjects of his kingdom is that we honestly and practically seek to obey the commands of the Lord Jesus Christ *out of love for the Saviour* and not legalism. In doing this our lives will change and we will become more like Christ. We will be seen to be his by this good fruit in our lives which ultimately cannot be counterfeited (Matthew 7:16-20).

THE APOSTLE PAUL:
THE THREE CHRISTIAN VIRTUES

Again and again in his letters the apostle Paul sets out three particular virtues which characterize real Christianity.

Look at 1 Corinthians 13:13; Colossians 1:5; 1 Thessalonians 1:3. What are the three virtues which mark the saving grace of God in our lives?

____

The writer of the epistle to the Hebrews may not have been Paul, but look up Hebrews 6:9-12. As he speaks of the 'things that accompany salvation', he emphasizes the same three virtues. How long does he say these virtues last in the Christian life?

____

____

____

How do these three virtues relate to our Lord's teaching on the marks of grace in the Sermon on the Mount?

____

____

____

Read Galatians 5:22-23. How do these three virtues relate to Paul's teaching on the fruit of the Spirit?

____

____

____

THE APOSTLE JOHN

John wrote his first letter in order that people might be assured that they really were saved Christian people (1 John 5:13).

How does John make it very clear that no Christian is perfect in this life? (1 John 1:8-10)

If the Christian falls into sin, what must he do? (1 John 1:7; 2:1-2)

However, having made it clear that Christians may not be perfect, John tells us that every Christian is marked by a changed life. The Christian is a changed person intellectually, morally and socially. His mind, will and affections have been transformed. This shows that the grace of God is in a person's life.

The Christian's *mind* has changed — he believes in Christ. Check what John says in 1 John 3:23; 4:15; 5:1, 5.

The Christian's *will* has been changed — the overall direction of his life is against sin and towards obedience. Check this in 1 John 2:3-6; 3:6, 9; 5:18.

The Christian's *affections* have changed — he loves God and loves other Christians. Check this in 1 John 2:10; 3:14; 4:7, 19-21.

All this shows the presence of the Holy Spirit in our lives (1 John 3:24; 4:13).

How does this teaching about the change of mind and will and heart in the Christian match up with what we saw about the Fall of man in Study 5?

THE LETTER OF JAMES

Look at James 2:14-26. According to James how does genuine faith show itself in someone's life?

Some people try to make out that James is contradicting Paul's great emphasis that we are saved by faith alone (Romans 3:28). But he is not. The truth is that Paul and James are addressing two slightly different questions. Paul is dealing with the question, 'How can sinners be saved?' His answer is, through faith in Christ and his merits alone. James, however, is addressing the question, 'How do we tell the difference between genuine faith and counterfeit presumption?' His answer is that genuine faith will always give rise to obedience and good works — not by way of trying to merit salvation, for James acknowledges that salvation is by faith (James 2:5), but simply because the Christian trusts and loves God.

Look at Galatians 5:6. How does this verse show that Paul agrees with James?

___

___

___

THE APOSTLE PETER

Look at 2 Peter 1:5-11. How does Peter relate the change in a person's life and growth in Christian character to God's decree of election?

___

___

___

___

See also 1 Peter 1:15-16.

How does Peter's call to Christians to seek to live holy lives now link up with the purpose for which we have been chosen by God? (Ephesians 1:4)

___

___

___

Thus we see that although the workings of the Holy Spirit within our hearts are secret and invisible, yet salvation shows itself in concrete ways in changed lives.

Conclusion

How would you summarize the New Testament's teaching on the marks of grace in the Christian's life?

____

____

____

____

What does it mean about us if we find that an honest look at our lives reveals that they are no different from those of people in the world?

____

____

If we find ourselves in this position we are not without hope, but what must we do?

____

____

____

STUDY 11
PRESERVATION AND PERSEVERANCE

We have seen that the Bible is from God and is fundamentally about God. It also tells us about man. It tells us that although man was originally made great in the image of God, he is now totally fallen and is unable to save himself or even to see his need.

God, in eternity, chose to save a great host from rebellious mankind. For these elect sinners Christ made atonement on the cross. In turn, God effectually calls each one of them and brings them to faith in Christ and thus into the experience of salvation.

The Christian continues on to the end of the journey.

A vital thing we need to realize is that God does not now lose any of those whom he has chosen, bought and called (John 6:39). He *preserves* them and brings each one of them safely to heaven. He does this by ensuring that each true Christian *perseveres* in the way of Christ and continues in the faith to the end. The wonderful truth is no true Christian will ever be lost.

God the Father has purposed to save his people, for whom Christ died and whom the Holy Spirit brings to new birth. If one of those whom God has purposed to save fails to arrive in heaven, then the omnipotent God has been defeated and he is no longer omnipotent and he cannot be God!

Read Isaiah 46:9-10. What have we seen to be 'his good pleasure'?

____

____

If God did not fulfil this what would that imply about him?

____

____

Now look up Ephesians 1:11-12. What is the purpose of our salvation?

____

____

If we can be lost, then these verses are not true. But that is impossible!

God will not forsake his elect. To do this he would have to change, deny what he has decided and do something which would not stand forever. These three things God cannot do. Look up 2 Timothy 2:13 and Ecclesiastes 3:14. What is the attribute of God referred to in these verses?

____

____

Once it is realized that God is sovereign and that he has purposed to save his people, it becomes clear that all true Christians are eternally secure.

He has paid so much; it is unthinkable that he would waste the price. If his power can save the ungodly, it is sufficient to keep the godly!

C. H. Spurgeon says: 'You will not be lost, for he who owns you is able to keep you. If you were to perish who would be the loser? Why, he to whom you belong, and "ye are not your own", ye belong to Christ. My hope of being preserved to the end lies in this fact, that Jesus Christ paid far too much for me ever to let me go. Each believer cost him his heart's blood. Stand in Gethsemane, and hear his groans: then draw near and mark his bloody sweat, and tell me, will he lose a soul for whom he suffered thus? See him hanging on the tree, tortured, mocked, burdened with an awful load, and then beclouded with the eclipse of his Father's face, and do you think he suffered all that and yet will permit those for whom he endured it to be cast into hell? He will be a greater loser than I shall if I perish, for he will lose what cost him his life: surely he will never do that. Here is your security, you are the Lord's portion, and he will not be robbed of his heritage. We are in a hand that bears the scar of the nail; we are hidden in the cleft of a rock — a rock that was riven for us near nineteen hundred years ago. None can pluck us from the hand that redeemed us; its pressure is too warm with love and strong with might for that.' [16]

ALTHOUGH COUNTERFEIT CHRISTIANS CAN AND WILL BE LOST A TRUE CHRISTIAN NEVER CAN

Sometimes the Scriptures speak of those who come under the umbrella of the church being eventually lost, but it always makes it clear that although these people had a semblance of faith, in fact they had never truly surrendered to Christ and were not real Christians.

Read the Parable of the Sower in Mark 4:1-20. Who are the real Christians and who are the 'temporary Christians'?

___

___

___

Look at verses 16-19. What are the reasons that these 'temporary Christians' give up on the faith?

___

___

___

Whatever their experience of the gospel, they had never so surrendered to Christ that no matter the hardships or other attractions that came along they would cling to him. Their heart of hearts had never really been changed. They were not Christians at all.

Read Hebrews 6:4-12. This passage speaks of the falling away of those who have had some kind of experience of the Holy Spirit. How does the writer describe their religious experience before their turning back?

These people are counterfeit Christians. The writer goes on to explain that true Christians experience better things — 'things that accompany salvation'. How does he show that he believes that where the marks of grace are truly evident that person will never be lost?

SPECIFIC BIBLE TEXTS TEACH THAT THE CHRISTIAN IS ETERNALLY SECURE

1. Some texts assert God's preservation of us. Look up these references and identify what *God* will do: John 6:37-39; Philippians 1:6; 1 Thessalonians 5:23-24; 2 Timothy 4:18.

2. Some texts confirm our security before God as our Judge. See Romans 8:31-34. Why can no one lay a charge against us?

See Jude 24-25. What is God able to do?

3. Some texts confirm our security through the faithfulness of God. See Hebrews 6:17-18.

   What are the two unchangeable things that give us comfort and certainty?

4. Some texts establish the nature of our life in God. What is the promise in John 11:26 and John 10:28-29?

   Look at 1 Peter 1:23. What is imperishable and what does that imply?

5. Some texts underline the inevitable fulfilment of God's purposes. Read Romans 8:30.

   Can you find any trace of uncertainty here?

   Read through Romans 8:37-39. List the things which are unable to cut us off from God. Does the list cover everything?

6. Some texts underline our endurance in the faith. See Romans 1:17.

   What will happen to the righteous, made righteous through faith?

See 1 John 5:18. Who keeps those whose lives are no longer dominated by sin?

THE BIBLICAL TERMS WHICH DESCRIBE SALVATION MAKE CLEAR THIS TRUTH OF THE BELIEVER'S PRESERVATION

1. Eternal life. Read John 3:15-16. How does this show that a Christian cannot be lost?

   Look at John 17:1-3. How does eternal life differ from eternal death?

   Eternal life does not just mean life of infinite duration but life of a different quality, like God's life. Eternal death is not annihilation, but eternal punishment (Matthew 25:46).

2. The pictures of Christians being Christ's bride (Ephesians 5:22-32), his temple building (Ephesians 2:19-22) and members of his body (Ephesians 1:22-23) all show that we are inextricably united to him who is the eternal One, for his eternal praise.

   How do these verses show that believers are eternally secure?

3. We are also pictured as being sons of God and brothers of Christ. As long as Christ lives and is, we are in favour with God.

   Read Romans 8:14-17. How do we know that we are sons of God?

   Look at Ephesians 1:4-6. Can anyone who is now 'in Christ' ever be unacceptable to God?

Conclusion

Christians can never be lost. God will bring us safe into the new heavens and earth. This truth is a cause of unspeakable comfort to God's children. If you are a child of the living God do not live like an orphan! Walk in fellowship with your Father. The truth of eternal security does not mean that we take salvation for granted and live ungodly lives: we show that we are children of God through godliness — and what a privilege it is! The only fitting conclusion is to bow humbly in worship and thanksgiving for the great grace God has shown towards us.

Home at last.

REFERENCES

1. *Works of Richard Sibbes*, edited by Alexander B. Grosart, Vol.1, Banner of Truth Trust, 1973 reprint, p.413.
2. Thomas Watson, *A Body of Divinity*, Banner of Truth Trust, 1975 reprint, p.14.
3. B. B. Warfield, *Selected Shorter Writings*, edited by John Meeter, Vol.1, Presbyterian and Reformed, 1970, p.104.
4. C. H. Spurgeon, *Metropolitan Tabernacle Pulpit*, Vol.33, Banner of Truth Trust, 1969 reprint, pp.198-199.
5. Richard Baxter, *Call to the Unconverted*, Evangelical Press, 1976 reprint, pp.42-43.
6. Martin Luther, *Sermons on the Gospel of St. John, Chapters 6-8* (trs. M. H. Bertram), Concordia Publishing House, St Louis, 1959, p.36.
7. B. B. Warfield, *The Plan of Salvation*, Eerdmans, revised edition, 1936, pp.73-74.
8. Cited in Henry Gariepy, *100 Portraits of Christ*, Victor Books, 1987, p.20.
9. *The Works of John Owen*, edited by William H. Goold, Vol.10, Banner of Truth Trust, 1967 reprint, p.285.
10. Matthew Poole, *A Commentary on the Holy Bible*, Vol.3, Banner of Truth Trust, 1963 reprint, p.921.
11. Gardiner Spring, *The Attraction of the Cross*, Banner of Truth Trust, 1983, p.34.
12. B. B. Warfield, *The Plan of Salvation*, pp.48-49.
13. B. B. Warfield, *Selected Shorter Writings*, Vol.2, p.726.
14. C. H. Spurgeon, *New Park Street Pulpit*, Vol.6, Banner of Truth Trust, 1964 reprint, p.256.
15. J. I. Packer, *Keep in Step with the Spirit*, Inter-Varsity Press, 1984, p.104.
16. C. H. Spurgeon, *Metropolitan Tabernacle Pulpit*, Vol.26, Banner of Truth Trust, 1971 reprint, p.476.